FEARNE COTTON

QUIET

Silencing the brain chatter and believing that
you're good enough

First published in Great Britain in 2018 by Orion Spring
This paperback edition first published in 2019 by Orion Spring
An imprint of Orion Publishing Group Ltd
Carmelite House, 50 Victoria Embankment, London, EC4Y 0DZ
An Hachette UK Company

1 3 5 7 9 10 8 6 4 2

A CIP catalogue record for this book is available from the British Library.

Mass Market Paperback ISBN: 9781409183150
Ebook ISBN: 9781409183167

Design: Hart Studio
Black and white illustrations: Fearne Cotton
Chapter illustrations: Jessica May Underwood
Activity illustrations and watercolour brain on inside cover: Hart Studio
Printed and bound in Great Britian by Clays Ltd, Elcograf, S.p.A

ORION
SPRING

www.orionbooks.co.uk

For Rex and Honey and all their noise

Introduction

I know, I know – the irony. A book called '*Quiet*' written by someone who talks for a living. Well, this is not a book about enforced silence or muting oneself, as of course I do love a bit of noise, whether it's the husk of Dave Grohl's voice blaring out of a speaker, my kids cracking up with laughter at each other or a crowd roaring with cheer and jubilation when someone incredible walks on to a stage. Noise can swell our emotions and inspire us to move, but I have also reached a point in my life where I really appreciate some quiet, too. Not just literal silence but also a mind free from negative Chatter and self-analysis. A quiet that comes from reducing that Chatter in our heads and having the confidence to ignore it. As you may know, I love a good chat, so try and imagine what is going on upstairs in my brain! At times it's like a UN peace negotiation up there. Toing and froing, bartering and convincing, constant ideas and worries. It's non-stop! That's why, over the last few years especially, finding the tools to switch off the noise and find the quiet has been so important to me, and I hope that can be important to you, too.

Quiet: A State of Mind

This book is certainly not about committing to a decade of silence while seeking out a woodland dwelling to retreat to in order to block out the modern world. It's about taming the much louder and cerebral beast that lives within the confines of our own skulls: this bad inner Chatter. We all know it has the power to overthrow gut instinct, shout us down when we are faced with fear and talk us out of new adventures – yet few of us have a grip on it. We will all suffer from a chattery brain to varying degrees and I'm sure most of us would love to know how to turn down the volume on it all so we can focus better, feel less anxious and try new things in life – I know I would! This is where the 'quiet' comes in. That space and clarity that allows us to acknowledge those thoughts and that inner dialogue yet not take every word seriously.

The 'quiet' is a slice of time in between thought and action where we can make a decision that isn't based purely on what the negative Chatter is telling us. It is an inner knowledge that we understand our own thought patterns but know we don't have to be ruled by them. Within the quiet we can act more intuitively and go with our guts and hearts to make decisions that feel authentic and positive. If we learn to find this quiet, we can hone in on how we really feel, as we aren't muddled by the negative thoughts and patterns we are so used to slipping into.

Quiet is a state of mind and one that requires a little discipline and effort. It's of course much easier to stay in habitual patterns, even if they are negative, as we are used to them. So to tune in to the much-needed quiet we need to put a little work in. I'm giving it a jolly good go alongside you, so will be cheerleading you along the way, as well as offering up some methods and theories I've learned so far.

The Chatter

So what exactly do I mean by the 'Chatter'? It's the negative stuff: what can sometimes feel like a constant barrage of head noise that often tries to take us down. It's the shitty names we call ourselves, the stories we play over again and again in our heads which we believe define who we are, the labels we assume others have given us that leave us feeling alienated, phrases that play on a loop when we're scared that have the ability to aggravate and coax out every tricky emotion. Little of this Chatter is true but that doesn't stop us from noticing it and act-ing accordingly. Our brains are of course capable of so much brilliance:

thoughts and ideas bubbling up like a shaken bottle of pop; mental exploration and expansion that can lead to great change and kindness and empathy towards others. Yet we also allow thoughts to hold us back and keep us spinning in cycles of mental pain.

Of course, this Chatter isn't heard with our ears but is clear as day in our minds. You may hear your own voice as the inner dialogue rambles on; a cinematic version of it, narrating your life as it plays out. Perhaps it is just thoughts and images that you scroll through mentally, bringing up the negative or feared – like an Instagram feed of your life. We might not be able to drown out the Chatter, or lose it for good, but I do believe if we take it much less seriously and remind ourselves that these thoughts are just one version of a story rather than hard facts, we can start to live alongside it with much more ease.

I'll give you an example. Whenever I walk into a room at a party, full of people I know, sort of know and don't know at all, I instantly assume, due to the negative dialogue rabbiting away upstairs in my head, that everyone in that room thinks I'm a twat. I can hear the mental Chatter starting up immediately, telling me that everyone is smarter, cooler and definitely doesn't have a Tupperware of crackers in their bag in case they get hungry later. BUT wait – if I can find my way into the quiet, then I can remember this narrative is just

ONE version of events. Maybe SOME people don't like me, but that doesn't mean that everyone doesn't. Maybe I will make a new friend – or help out a hungry pre-existing friend with the aforementioned snacks. The negative Chatter isn't based on fact. It's assumption, fantasy and, for me, usually a little self-torture, too.

We Are All Experts

Much like with my other books, *Happy* and *Calm*, I do not profess to have this one down pat (clearly, from that last anecdote). I do not exclusively work from positivity or the gut and have yet to master how to rid myself of that negative dialogue we all seem to weirdly cling to. I'm very much at the bottom of the ladder with this one, but in the last couple of years I have climbed up a rung or two due to the fact that I can now easily notice when these aggravating voices spark up. I can weed out the crap-talking, confidence-thwarting Chatter from the authentic wisdom that is in there somewhere. We are all brimming with inner wisdom and are naturally experts in our specialist subject: ourselves. Yet we allow the negative thoughts and dialogue to confuse us. We forget how capable we are, how strong we can be and how deep we have dug before. There is confidence there

even if it's hidden; there is courage, beauty, wisdom and belief – we just need some quiet to notice it.

Taking Back Control

Negative Chatter doesn't yield more power than our propensity to think positively but we are all so used to letting it have its way. You know those moments when your initial reaction to an opportunity is one of excitement but half an hour later you've talked yourself out of it? The inner cheerleader and gut said a big fat 'YES' and then the mental Chatter came out to play, kicking a large ball of self-doubt right in the gut to wind us and deflate our inner joy and confidence.

Chatter deals in assumption and fear. Our negative thoughts are usually based on what we fear in the future or the past and not about what is currently and truly going on around us. That exam you're freaked out about that is causing an influx of self-doubt and a dialogue that tells you you're not good enough is all based on a fear of the future. A fear that you'll panic in the exam, not think clearly and then fail to answer any of the questions presented to you. That negative Chatter telling you you're too chatty/wobbly/nervous/unattractive which you hear every time you meet a new potential partner is purely based on the past. Snippets you have assumed or possibly heard others say about you that you have applied to the present. It's not based on reality or fact, just the fear of the past. The reality is that we are all good enough, capable and deserving of good fortune – we just need a little quiet to remember it.

I think when we truly know something is real, a good decision or something just feels right, there is very little talk in the mind at all. Love, acceptance, healing, help, balance, calm – the feelings that tingle and vibrate through our solar plexus – don't need words to articulate their worth or power. They are simply felt.

Resurfacing Our Inner Wisdom

We hear so many tones of Chatter and they are different for each of us. Depending on what we have experienced so far in our lives, the mental Chatter will work with what it is given. It will find a way to be noticed when our Achilles' heel flares up. Your own weaknesses or fears might relate to relationships, work, trust, family, confidence, sex, creativity. Whatever they are, there will be some Chatter thrown into the mix that tests you and stretches you and, more often than not, confuses the hell out of you. Our overactive brains just don't know when to stop.

I imagine this has all gotten a lot worse in the last decade or so, too. We are presented with more imagery, faster-paced TV shows, more expectation to achieve more in a single day, a plethora of ways to connect, reconnect and engage. We are taught that anything other than a fast-paced life is foolish – or perhaps 'less than'. We know more about other people and have more reason to compare ourselves to others. We hear news from every corner of the planet and can get what we want online in seconds. We think doing things quickly saves time whereas it is, in fact, stopping us from enjoying the time we have. It is hard in this environment not to become one big melting pot of thoughts, fears and worries that are made up partly of personal experience, but also partly of what the modern world is projecting back at us. How on earth do we collectively stay sane and also stay connected to what we believe to be true? If there was ever a time for us to concentrate on this, it is now.

I hope in this book to use my own anecdotal truth, as well as interviews with great friends and incredible experts, to illustrate how and when I have noticed the negative Chatter creep on in. Maybe that'll open you up to noticing what your own mental Chatter sounds like and when it is most prevalent. Then we can begin to mitigate its uninhibited and unwelcome influence. Understanding our Chatter and how it affects each one of us allows us to have more confidence in situations we feel are uncomfortable, giving us maximum opportunity to thrive in the most exuberant way and helping us make decisions when we feel utterly stuck.

The Power of Positive Thoughts

One way I believe we can mitigate the power of Chatter and find our way to quiet is with positive thought. Mantras, affirmations, inner pep talks – whatever you want to call them, they can help out big time if you learn to use them properly and practise them, like you have subconsciously done with negative names and phrases. They may be harder to conjure up at first, as they're unfamiliar and feel untrue, but, of course, they can become a lot more familiar over time when we remember to prioritise them over the negative. The default Chatter might be 'I am awful/ugly/useless/pathetic', but we can learn to switch it up to 'I am unique/beguiling/capable/strong' with a little discipline and effort (and perhaps clenched bum cheeks, as us Brits are so awful at self-celebration).

The holy grail of Chatter busting, which this much needed positive thought will help us ascend to, is 'the quiet'. A place where negative thoughts may still occasionally lurk but where we have the confidence to let them drift in and out so they have little impact on our decisions. A state of mind which allows us to think clearly in a grounded, connected and loving way. Not only does decision-making become slicker in this headspace but we are open to what is really going on around us. We become firmly planted in the moment, so much so that fantasy and assumption dissipate into the blurry background. We are too focused on the present and real to give any time of day to the absurd negative Chatter we accidentally click into. It might seem unreachable to permanently be in the quiet, as we are, of course, all fallible and often tired and fatigued, but to know we can get there in times of need is a comfort in itself.

Let's get this Chatter under control together and learn to trust our poor drowned-out intuition so we make good choices, believe in ourselves and delve in to the new and adventurous in life!

The Triggers

Can you instantly think of situations that ignite your inner negative Chatter? Is it thinking of future plans on the horizon or does it latch on to moments in your past? For me, it's a little of both. I conflate information I believe to be true and end up in a vortex of negative thinking. I call this my 'spiral'. I spiral quite a bit and the triggers are always the same:

- I usually have quite a lot of anxiety around what people think of me. Now, deep down, I know I don't really care, but my negative Chatter gives me reason to ignore my gut feelings. It prefers an elaborate and dramatic dialogue about how horrendous everyone thinks I am. So meeting new people or approaching new situations or jobs are among my triggers. They can hinder me from using my inner courage and trust.

- Spending too long on social media is another, due to the afore-mentioned assumption that everyone thinks I'm an arsehole. Reading what others think of us is now more readily available due to social media and this can of course heighten our negative thought patterns. The Chatter loves this one as other people's thoughts are presented in black and white so seem more potent and perhaps impactful, too. Sometimes I'm in autopilot mode, scrolling through other people's thoughts and images that I really don't need in my head, and I forget to observe what I'm doing and thinking.

- Thinking of times when I have fucked up is a huge one for me. I may have a random memory of something or someone else brings a past moment up in conversation and, all of a sudden, I'm flummoxed. My negative Chatter goes into overdrive and sucks the past up like a hoover before coughing it all up into my present. I often feel I am actually IN the past in these moments so the Chatter brings along a lot of emotion and feeling, too. Stagnant and redundant feelings that no longer serve me swarm my every cell and seem impossible to shake. This is a real confidence crusher and is in no way conducive to loving oneself.

- Failing is a tough one for everyone and definitely something that keeps a steady dialogue of negativity rotating for days on end. I can waste whole weeks replaying sloppy words spoken or badly executed attempts at something and I know this holds me back massively. I become very stuck in the negative thought patterns, which hold me in a straightjacket of self-pity and fear, and prevent me from picking myself back up again.

- Getting run down or sick. When I can't be as proactive and determined as I normally like to be I spiral quickly. I like to be on the move, creating, brainstorming, exploring and when I can't the Chatter starts up. I call myself lazy and useless and worry that I'll never get momentum back again. Rather than sinking into some still and quiet, I get more angsty and fidgety.

- I'm not somebody who does lack of sleep well. My husband is amazing and can carry on regardless of how many hours were spent snoozing. I, on the other hand, turn into a grumpy, irritable, selfish grumble-pants, and consequently I'm consumed by the Chatter. An angry dialogue forms and I am full of self-pity and fear that I will not achieve what I had originally set out to do that day.

I have thought through each of the following chapter subjects carefully based on these triggers; hopefully you'll connect with each one and find my musings interesting and also helpful in abating the issues we are dealing with.

What are your triggers? Can you write some of them down here now? Is it a feeling of failure? Jealousy? Anger and injustice? Perhaps being overtired? It is a good place for us all to start so that we are aware of what causes those negative thought patterns and inner Chatter. Then we can start to combat it with some good old-fashioned positivity and a big lump of quiet!

....

....

....

....

....

....

....

....

....

....

....

....

....

....

Chatter: the Different Voices

There are many different strains of negativity that we experience on a daily basis. You may have ones I don't and vice versa, but in this book I'm going to willingly spill the beans on the ones I hear daily and battle with. Recognising the different shades of Chatter we experience allows us to gain more perspective on them and to work out how to turn them off. See if any of the below apply to your own life and inner dialogue.

☐ The Lazy One

The one that tells you not to bother going for that morning run/opening the bills piling up/calling that friend you haven't spoken to in ages. It will always think up elaborate and silly excuses.

☐ The Inner Critic One

I'm pretty sure we all have this one! It picks holes in our every move, especially when we feel we haven't done our best.

☐ The Catastrophising One

This one panics that we have left a candle on, which will in turn burn the house down. It conjures up images of loved ones in horrific situations simply because they didn't answer your phone call. It runs on vivid imagination and the worst-case scenario.

☐ The Naysayer One

This one assumes you'll fail at whatever you try. It holds us back and doesn't want us to attempt anything new in case of failure and looming embarrassment.

☐ The Evil One

This one tells us we are a piece of shit. It compares us to others and highlights mistakes from the past to send us down a path of total self-loathing.

☐ The Over-Congratulatory One

This one can be hard to admit. The voice that uses ego to tell us we are better than others or know more. It can be defensive and arrogant and stops us from learning. It hinders us from seeing other perspectives and blinkers us from newness.

☐ The Angry One

This voice replays moments of injustice or frustration and rants and raves what you could have and should have said. It manifests physically if we are not careful, as the words so desperately want to be released.

☐ The Childlike One

This voice keeps us stuck in the past with a whining sing-song 'it's not fair'. It is tantrum-like and stops us from looking at lessons we could learn in tough times.

☐ The Voice of Others

A sly trickster of a voice that comes from conflated information spoken by others yet masquerades as our own thoughts. It tells us we are useless because someone else once said it. It says we can't do something because someone else once told us we can't.

☐ The FOMO One

A very millennial new voice that looks around too much at what others are doing and tells us we are not having enough fun – it's literally a Fear of Missing Out. Thoughts bubble up, telling us we aren't 'living our best life' – whatever the hell that means.

☐ The Game-Playing One

This mind Chatter tells us that if we make the next green traffic light everything will be okay. It is superstitious and latches on to weird idiosyncrasies to forge a fantasy outcome.

Tick the boxes next to any of the Voices that you experience and then add in any other ones that you would like to silence below. Name them and get to know the traits of each inner voice so they're easy to spot.

....

....

....

....

....

....

....

....

....

1

Quiet Observation

I ruminated on which chapter and subject to begin with and landed on 'Quiet Observation' because I think we must first start with awareness. This is the part where we take a little self-inventory and time to reflect on how our own bespoke Chatter works. Maybe this is the first time you've given your own Chatter a thought? Perhaps this is your first step towards thinking of this ongoing background noise as something that isn't necessarily true? This is what this part of the book is all about. Taking note of your own negative thought patterns and joining the dots as to why they spark up.

In the Beginning

We will all, to some extent, be governed by a negative voice, or chorus of negative voices, during our lifetime. You may recall this Chatter beginning as a child or perhaps when you entered the daunting world of secondary school, further education or work. Perhaps the Chatter always pipes up when you're nervous or even over-excited. Maybe it comes and goes as you surf the peaks and troughs of your own human existence.

I count myself very lucky that I grew up in a very non-dramatic fashion. I went to school, hung out with my mates in the local park and watched my mum and dad both work extremely hard to give us sunny camping holidays in France and the odd fancy trip to Center Parcs. I had very little scope on others' opinions of me and self-doubt was yet to rear its scaly head.

I think most children live very much in the moment and react according to what is happening around them. If they feel hard done by, they shout and scream and lie on the floor, writhing about in the hope that the poor bedraggled parent nearby will give in to the theatre production of tears and pass over the much desired choc ice. If they are happy, they'll skip freely without inhibition and sing at the top of their voices to express the glee pulsating round their bodies. Worrying about what others think or even remembering and applying previous moments of reprimanding or warning is just not an option to most kids. We drift close to the things that make us feel good and naturally shy away or bolt from those that don't.

I feel fortunate to have been one of these free, tantrum-prone, over-excitable kids, like many of you will have been, too. I think only when a young person has been affected by trauma or shock will they perhaps deviate from this kind of behaviour.

So when does the inhibition-free world of childhood stop and self-awareness start? I'm sure it can be very different for all of us and perhaps it can start a lot younger these days now kids are exposed to social media and the internet. You may remember the exact moment when you first felt like you were different or didn't belong or perhaps were not good enough. I think this kicked in for me a little later than expected – which I feel fortunate about. I got my foot in the sequin-covered showbiz door aged 15 and loved every minute. I was young, impressionable and, of course, naive. Name me a teenager who isn't! I skipped into the studio each day with my head full of lines learned and my practised happy-go-lucky smile. I felt like I had been plucked from suburban obscurity to do a job that was overwhelmingly exciting and other-worldly. Prior to this seminal career moment, I had been sashaying my way through dance school on a 4/5-day basis outside of my regular state school and dreaming big.

The atmosphere at my local dance and drama club was joyful and never bordered on nasty or competitive. We all had each others' lycra-clad backs and wanted to see one another succeed. Big shout out to Soul Performing Arts School in Ruislip. I have such gorgeous memories from this era: productions of *Bugsy Malone* in our local theatre, and street dance shows at Earls Court Olympia for the big yearly dance exhibitions. We were a collective mass of motivation and high hopes. I felt part of a gang and one which could laugh, sweat and take a chance without judgement or mockery.

Imposter Syndrome

Starting my first job at *Disney Club*, and then *Diggit* on ITV, opened up a whole new world that I really wasn't equipped for. I loved it and all the people I worked with were beyond supportive and nurturing, but my own mind began a new dialogue and one that I wasn't sure how to handle.

A year or so into my broadcasting career I found myself regularly sat next to a lithe, perfect-haired, confident pop star around my age, which instantly opened me up to self-comparison for the first time ever. I had slouched my way through high school unscathed, as I had a group of amazing mates who are still my besties to this day, and then split-leaped through my local dance and drama school with the aforementioned joy. This feeling of comparison was all new.

Get ready for some cracking 90s references: each week I would interview Samantha Mumba, with her endless legs, or Billie Piper, with her mature nature and calm approach. Some weeks Girl Thing would grace our studio, with their matching outfits and straight white teeth, and in others, Cleopatra would burst onto the set with their neon eye shadow and perfectly honed stomach muscles. I felt like a complete imposter. I had chubby round cheeks (which by the way I now look back and am very fond of) and a fringe I had cut myself, legs that always felt too muscly and bulky under my purple chord flares (I know, so cool!) and was too eager to fill moments of silence with over-excitable laughter. How were they all so cool and calm and confident and how were they refusing all of the free toasted cheese sandwiches on arrival to the studio? I was sure they could recognise this 'lacking' in me, too. Looking back there was nothing wrong with the young, greasy-fringed, slightly overwhelmed 15-year-old Fearne – and I'm sure Samantha, Billie and the rest were thinking the same – but at the time I felt odd. The negative voices had sparked up. The Chatter that would tell me I

wasn't good enough and shouldn't be there in the first place. The whisper that might grow into a shout telling me that everyone else had life so sorted and yet I didn't.

Luckily my naivety and general joy did not allow these voices to ruin the experience for me at all. I'm not sure they even held me back as I was so hell bent on having this new career work out, but they were definitely there. I'm actually rather envious of how I was naturally able to mitigate this Chatter's self-indulgence as I probably have a tougher time working with it now in my late thirties. Perhaps that ability was due to the little bit of childlike spontaneity I still had, allowing me to stay more in the moment and to quickly forget the content of my negative thoughts? Remembering that I used to be naturally quite good at doing this gives me great hope that I will be so again. I'm sure you can think back to moments where you have overcome the Chatter in your own way, too. More on this later.

HELLO TO . . . BILLIE PIPER

Looking back at that era of my life brings so much joy. It wasn't a traumatic time or particularly heavy, there was just a lot of newness which made me much more aware of my own thought patterns and feelings. I love reminiscing and thinking about my beloved Buffalo trainers and harsh fringe and the people I met along the way. One of those shiny popstars went on to become an established actress and theatre performer with such elegance and grace: Billie Piper. Billie's career took off at exactly the same time as mine. She was the kooky, smart pop girl, with a washboard stomach and award-winning smile, who I so loved interviewing. She was our own answer to Britney Spears and young enough and cool enough to feel like the best friend we all wanted. My mental Chatter would very much make me believe that she was much more mature and savvy than I was – and I was always slightly in awe of how she handled the crazy fame and lifestyle her career offered up. We've kept in touch a little over the years so I thought it would be a nice opportunity to turn back time and look at the crazy pop-tastic 90s and how Billie was really feeling on the inside at that time.

F: Billie, we started our professional lives around the same time 8,000 years ago. I remember so clearly interviewing you for the first time. I was wearing awful bunches in my hair and had on an unflattering fleece hoodie and you looked super cool and appeared to be very calm and collected in that space. How did you feel starting work so young?

B: I think we both wore a lot of fleece in that period! Fleece gilets and bunches. I thought you were the super-established one of us both. Smart, cool and always beautiful inside and out. There's a lot about that time that I'm deeply grateful for now. But there's no doubt I could have seen and enjoyed that lifestyle and those opportunities more a number of years later. There were a few years where I was not remotely calm and if it appeared that way it was probably an act. In fact I felt quite the opposite. I couldn't deal with the fame whatsoever – I became extremely controlling and reclusive. The silver lining is that I went into the next phase of my life and career in a much more measured way. Having said that, it's only now in my mid-thirties that I feel truly rested – and even then I have my moments.

F: Luckily neither of us had to deal with the onslaught of social media at that tender age, which I'm forever grateful for, but we did get feedback and have a rough idea of what others thought about us. How did that affect your own self-worth early on?

B: I was headstrong and ambitious as a young girl, but when I read about what people thought of me and my appearance I started to unravel a bit and became especially fixated on my weight. Thank god for the absence of social media. I don't know how the hell young girls and boys are coping – or their parents. I worry sick about my kids showing an interest in it and being of age. Whatever that is.

F: As you've aged and gathered experience, how has your self-worth changed?

B: My self-worth relies almost exclusively on how well I'm taking care of myself. I've learnt this in the last two years.

F: What does your own negative mental Chatter sound like? What do you beat yourself up about or berate yourself about?

B: 'You're a stupid bitch', 'you should care more', 'you shouldn't be at work, you should only ever be with your kids', 'you don't want things enough', 'you want things too much', 'you're fat – your face is weird' – nice and chilled stuff like that! We call it 'the after party' in our friend circle.

F: The after party! I love that. (P.S. you have the best face.) Your career has been extraordinary and you've achieved so much, but I'm sure like most out there you still have wobbles? How do you deal with any negative feedback that gets thrown your way?

B: I avoid reading anything about what people think of me. I keep my life small. I focus on what's important to me. I only ever work on things I really, really care about. I accept what I'm not good at and I try and go into things open-armed. I also have a lot of therapy.

F: Do you ever take on outside commentary as your own and confuse the voice of others with your own?

B: Not at the moment. Thanks to the love of my family and boyfriend and again – the therapy.

F: Do you like/love yourself?

B: This stuff I struggle with because it makes me cringe and it's not how I was raised. Self-love or self-like is only obvious in how much I take care of myself. When I'm doing that I realise that in some way I'm loving myself.

F: What bits of yourself do you find it hard to love or even accept?

B: My feet.

F: Thank you so much Billie. I'm so in awe of what you've achieved and look forward to seeing what wonders you conjure up next!

Why So Serious?

One of the main problems with this Chatter is not necessarily that it is happening to us, but more importantly that we take it very seriously and don't always notice the effect it is having on different pockets of our lives. A personal example may help illustrate this. I have quite a large metaphorical mirror reflecting back at me in the working portion of my life. I can see on Instagram, Twitter or hear from general feedback when bumping into passers-by just how my work is perceived. I can then make the decision on whether to digest this information or park it altogether. Usually I gobble it down quickly and get indigestion of the mind.

One person may have thought my outfit that day was strange. One may feel the need to tell me they prefer one of my peers. One may have loved the words I spoke that day. One may have laughed at my views on life. There will be a plethora of thoughts shining back at me in all their glory. Now there is no rule saying that I have to believe any of these opinions and there is certainly no proof that the opinions of others, whether negative or positive, are fact – so why do I take them all so very seriously? Why does my negative mental Chatter tell me I must take them all on board?

It's perhaps a concoction of The Voice of Others and my inner Naysayer telling me I shouldn't dare to be positive. Personally, I have to remember that this Chatter has been created by my overthinking mind and if I tune in to what I know deep down is real, then I am okay. I'm still going to be okay if Bob from Birmingham thinks I'm a twat. I'm still going to be okay if Michelle from Highgate didn't like my outfit. That is what I authentically and intuitively know deep down. When I peel back the layers of Chatter that coat my mind in a grimy fog, I know that it doesn't really matter. I don't have to take it all so seriously. This requires a step back, a moment, a shard of clarity to separate me from the fantasy. Some quiet. I am me, I am okay and this Chatter is passing thoughts and not my reality.

Look Who's Talking

As well as not taking it all so seriously, we must remember that the opinions of others don't have to then become our own. We mustn't let things we have heard about ourselves rewrite our own story and redefine who we are. Of course there is a fine line as we will all receive warranted criticism that could be useful. In these circumstances, we can choose to take on board another's opinion and perhaps act on it, if it feels right, but without it devaluing what we already know about ourselves. This fine line can be distinguished by seeking out some quiet. When we sift out that Chatter and perhaps go for a walk, or take 5 minutes to just let information digest, then we can locate what our intuition is telling us. Is there some constructive truth in what the other person is saying or were they saying it in a judgemental way? Then we can react with dignity, knowing that this new information won't deeply affect us long term and could actually be quite useful. The Over-Congratulatory Voice does not like this sort of situation. It does not want to be told home truths or even get advice. It is a know-it-all and keeps us in very defensive thought patterns. Noticing that others have an opinion and how that informs our mental Chatter is important as it gives us a clear distinction between opinion and the truth: our truth.

It can swing both ways, too. We may have been told by another that we are so unbelievably knowledgeable about economics or plied with compliments for our ability to work quickly. The Over-Congratulatory Voice in our heads might try to twist these outside thoughts into fuel for our egos. If we enter a conversation about money and our mind Chatter enters the scene to sneer, 'Ha, remember I know the most about money round here – this lot are amateurs', then we are more than likely going to be shut off from other people's thoughts and ideas, thereby missing out on interesting and educational stuff. We might cut someone off as they're speaking as we believe our opinion on the subject is far more valuable and pertinent.

If we are working in a team, and pride ourselves on speed, our negative Chatter might attempt an arrogant elevation to look down on others and keep us from truly connecting with people. We may miss out on what is really going on around us or perhaps think badly of those who work at a slower pace. In these moments, the Chatter encourages us to appear lofty and grandiose and of course much louder than others so it can get its supposedly superior point across. This is not to say that we shouldn't buck the clichéd Brit behaviour and take gorgeous compliments on board, just that we mustn't let our mental Chatter lead us into the trap of believing we are always right. We can distinguish real knowledge and the power of what we believe vs getting on our high horse about something due to our negative Chatter. This is what makes spotting this Chatter tricky. It can masquerade as a bit of a cheerleader but the outcome can be judging others if it's coming from a bad place. If we can see how ephemeral and unimportant these voices in our heads are in both a negative situation and a positive one, then we can start to work out how we truly feel about our own lives and where we are heading.

Write from the Heart

One method I find instantly helpful to wheedle out the real from the Chatter is to write. If you have read any of my other books or listened to my podcasts, you'll know I bang on about the joys of writing a fair bit. Sometimes when we sit in solitary silence, mulling over the inner workings of our own brains, we get confused. Trying to unpick all of this Chatter in our heads alone can seem like an insurmountable challenge. When we have a conversation with a friend we might self-edit to protect ourselves from embarrassment and shame.

Writing stuff down allows us to dissect openly and freely instead. I like to grab a pen and a notepad (I have a real thing for stationery) and let my hand move quickly and freely without too much thought. The outcome is always interesting and very revealing as I realise how I really feel about a situation. Anger I was physically feeling can turn out, in reality, to be sadness. The Angry Voice inside may have been making me feel fiery about a subject, whereas what was actually afoot was a deep need to feel accepted. On reflection, I can then start to read between the lines. I can make more sense from it all and route back to the 'whys' without the constant Chatter butting in. Why do I feel angry? Is it how I really feel or am I allowing the Chatter to confuse matters by getting involved? Why do I feel stressed out? Am I allowing the Chatter to take the reins again? Seeing everything laid out on lined paper makes this particular Virgo feel a lot more in control. Give it a try if it feels right to you.

No one is watching or judging. The pen acts as a channel – it filters out the bullshit and sifts out the gold. Only the truth will fit through the thin pointy end of that pen, so the Chatter has to take a back seat.

Talk It Out

If I really can't see the wood for the trees, I will look for a connection. Now as you've just read, I often feel I self-edit when talking to reduce any unwanted feeling or labels I have put upon myself, but if I pick the right person (some would say 'victim' *sarcasm*) then I know I can let my brain unfurl and splurge out whatever it is that feels fit to burst from within it. Human connection is so important in moments of mental chaos. Again and again, I have been lucky enough to connect with some pretty special humans who have allowed me to offload without judgement or exaggerated reaction.

If the Catastrophising Voice is shouting loudly, I reach for the phone and speak to someone I trust. Do any of you lot let a Catastrophising

If you're in a negative head space, write down what the problem is within the tree. As you are writing, try to work out what the underlying problem is – the 'root' of the issue – and write these on the roots of the tree. Working out the real causes of our negativity helps us to accept it or find a remedy.

Voice send you spiralling on a perfectly lovely day? This voice might be telling me that everyone around me seems to be getting ill so it'll be me next. It could very well be, but I certainly don't need to be allowing this particular voice's potency to ruin a perfectly peaceful day when I could be putting my energies into helping those around me who are actually in physical ill health. There's a selfishness to this voice so I know I need to speak to another who can instil faith and hope into the mix.

Faith and hope are both beautiful feelings that permeate from our hearts when we remember they're there and aren't overshadowed by the Chatter. These emotions are not stored in the brain and have little to do with this Chatter at all. Having someone you know who deals in this 'realness' and has no time for the fantasy and drama in life is invaluable. Sometimes I just need a jolly good yank back down to earth as the Catastrophising Voice sends me rocketing into outer space. In these moments, I'm so far from the quiet that I could be enjoying. Another person has the ability to gently pull me closer to the ground and to what is really going on so I can observe these strange, dramatic thoughts, but not let them impact on my day or, indeed, health.

The great thing about being honest is that we realise how many other people feel similar. Our internal Chatter might convince us that everyone has it sorted and can cope just fine with life's weird twists and turns, but we can't. It's all bollocks. Once again, we need to take this voice less seriously and remember that at some point everybody on planet Earth without exception has felt scared, worried and unable to move forward. That there is connection. We are all in this together.

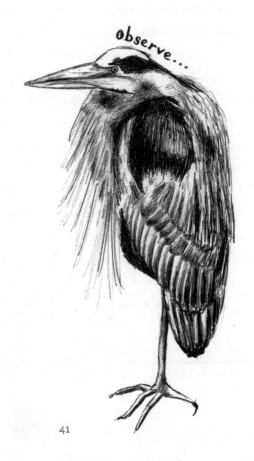

HELLO TO . . . SARAH MCKAY

Before I ramble on, I think I should introduce you to the marvellous Dr Sarah McKay. Sarah is a neuroscientist, director of the Neuroscience Academy and author of *The Women's Brain Book* and *Demystifying the Female Brain*. She studied at Oxford and loves to make understanding the brain accessible to everyone – which is a huge relief for people like me who can only hide behind six average GCSEs. Her website, Your Brain Health, is personable and easy to understand and gives such an insight into the complexities and inner workings of our brains. Sarah very kindly agreed to answer my questions on the Chatter so we can all get to grips with what exactly it is and why it's important to break negative thought patterns.

F: Sarah, let's cut to the chase. What on earth is going on in our brains when we hear all of these voices?

S: In the neuroscience and psychology world we call the negative voices within 'rumination'. The prefrontal cortex (as its name suggests) sits at the front of the brain behind your forehead, and is sometimes called the brain's CEO because it acts like a wise leader exerting top-down control over other brain areas – including emotional regulation and navigating complex social relationships. So the prefrontal cortex is responsible for rumination, but on the positive flip side, it's also capable of shutting down that rumination.

F: Is there a certain age or stage of development in our lives where rumination begins to happen in our brains? As kids we all seem very free and untinged by past experience and thought. What is happening in our brains as we age and gather more life experience and why does that lead to us over-analysing and worrying so much?

S: During adolescence, the deep brain structures involved with emotions start to mature and refine their function well before the prefrontal cortex matures. This 'developmental mismatch' between the prefrontal cortex and emotional brain is thought to be responsible for heightened emotional reactivity and negative thinking patterns during the teenage years.

Teenage girls in particular have a propensity to rumination, that is overthinking or mentally chewing over intense emotional experiences, their possible causes and consequences rather than actively coming up with a proactive solution. In adolescence, gender differences in the tendency to guilt and shame oneself emerge, and girls are especially focused on body dissatisfaction.

F: Are these voices made up from fragments of the past – memories that perhaps leave an imprint in our brains and come up when triggered?

S: Sometimes these voices may be made up from fragments of our past, or perhaps we just get stuck in a habitual negative thinking/ ruminating loop. Habitual negative thinking is rather like any other habit we develop. All habits have some common features. They are triggered by a specific event, thought or feeling, they are learned by repetition over time – in a sense you practise them till you perfect them and can perform them without effort.

F: Do you think this particular problem is much more prevalent in the modern world? We have so much more noise, stimulation, information available that perhaps our brains are slightly overloaded. Have our brains changed over time? Have physical changes occurred due to technology and the speed at which we live at? How did the brain differ, say, one hundred years ago to how it works now?

S: I haven't seen any evidence that our brains have changed over time due to the speed at which we live. However, there definitely are consequences for connecting via technology ONLY rather than face to face. Humans are social animals and our individual health and mental health depends on the health of the community. Social fragmentation and the fast pace of modern life leaving little time to connect slowly probably does impact us. We can easily feel isolated or begin to feel excluded and alienated, even when we may not be. Human connections work best when they're face to face or voice to voice. We can then rely on the rich nuance of facial expressions and tones and gestures. When we rely instead on social technology for communications we lose that nuance and richness.

F: This Inner Chatter can have a huge sway in our decision-making in life but it can also cause physical effects. Stress and worry can have a huge impact on our bodies. What actually happens during this transaction? How does thought transcend into the physical?

S: How stress gets under our skin is an excellent question and I write about it in my book in the chapter on mental health. We all respond to stress in different ways (some of that difference is biological and some due to life experiences) and whether one particular event is stressful varies from person to person. So what I may perceive as relatively benign, you might find incredibly threatening and it may elicit a biological stress response in you, not me, and vice versa. We feel 'stressed' when real or imagined pressures exceed our perceived ability to cope. Thus, dealing with stress requires access to practical, emotional and especially social resources to prop you up against the event. Sometimes it's not so much the actual event or thought itself, but how out of control it makes us feel.

There are two biological pathways that work in our bodies and brains to mediate stress response. The first is the sympathetic nervous system and the second is the hypothalamic-pituitary-adrenal axis, also known as the HPA axis. These two systems exist in our bodies to maintain physiological balance. The sympathetic nervous system acts as the frontline fight-or-flight responder and utilises adrenalin and noradrenalin. The HPA axis is slower to respond and longer lasting and utilises the hormone cortisol, which is made in the adrenal cortex of the adrenal glands which sit on top of the kidneys. Cortisol has an undeserved bad reputation. It's rather a Goldilocks hormone – you need just the right amount for good health. Too little or too much and you're at risk of health problems. Excess long-term stress is detrimental.

F: Do you have any personal tips for learning to live with these voices within, or how to accept that Chatter is simply thought and not reality?

S: Learning to regulate our emotions allows us to navigate complex and changing social landscapes and foster mental well-being. Being able to calmly assess and keep your emotions in check is a life skill. Emotional regulation skills don't magically appear as we become adults but they can be formally taught – we can be coached in cognitive reappraisal or challenging our thinking or feeling; it is a skill that can be learned!

The key to breaking these negative thinking patterns is to recognise the trigger and 'wire' in a new positive habit in place of the old. But this isn't always easy! Finding out the trigger can be hard and then performing the new positive behaviour can be hard and then practising over and over again is also rather hard. Like anyone, I too have had to battle those voices telling me I'm not good enough. I certainly battled with impostor syndrome when I started my PhD studies at Oxford University. One of the first steps in overcoming imposter syndrome for me was realising everyone experiences it (I heard even Barack Obama suffered from it, which I found comforting).

For me I have tried to apply neuroscience tactics, in particular what I understand about the neurobiology of habit formation. I know you can't unlearn or 'unwire' an old bad habit, rather you must mindfully learn or 'wire in' a new positive habit in its place based on the original trigger.

Oh, and a little counselling or therapy session never goes amiss! When I was having a particularly stressful time at the end of 2017 completing my book manuscript I decided to apply another principle I firmly believe in – the power of social connection. I joined an amateur dramatics group and we put on a spoof Eurovision musical as a fundraiser for my children's school. The new challenge, friendships, laughter and complete change of pace away from my desk alone writing a book were the balm I needed against the negative voices and stress.

F: Thank you so much, Sarah. It is invaluable to have this deeper understanding of what is really going on upstairs.

Being Present and Drowning Out the Voices

Do you ever have times when coincidences keep happening? I had one of these weeks just recently. These alignments can appear in the strangest of forms if you're open to them and mine were certainly a little left of centre. The first occurred when I was reading my daughter her bedtime stories. We have a huge long box of Mr Men books and on this particular night she pointed at the box and said, 'That one peeeeeease' with a small finger gesticulating towards the picture of Mr Messy, with his tangled pink hair and crazed eyes.

My first thought was, 'Bloody hell, how on earth am I going to locate this book quickly in my overtired state when all of the books are out of chronological order? I know . . . I'll pull a random one from the box of roughly 40 books and then convince her that it is a better story than Mr Messy's.'

I plucked a book two thirds along the length of spines and BLOODY HELL out came Mr Messy. I felt strangely chuffed and read the book with a little more enthusiasm than normal.

'ANOTHER,' Honey cried when we'd finished. 'THAT ONE

peeeeeease', pointing this time at Mr Nosy. 'Oh god, here we go again,' I thought. 'THIS time I'll pick at random and then wax lyrical about the content of the random "Mr" chosen.' I ran my fingers along the long row of books and plucked out Mr Nosy. WHAT THE ACTUAL . . . ! I'm no mathematician, so have no idea what the odds are on picking two of these books out of 40 in a row, but I wonder if I managed it because I was being open, listening and observing without realising. In other words, I was present. I was perhaps having a moment, perhaps a day or a week where I was being a little more present – and a bit more immune to negative mind Chatter. Or maybe I am the new Dynamo? As trivial as a Mr Man selection process may seem, I think it's important to be open to these signs.

The Chatter can stop us from seeing or hearing the signs. It shuts shop and stops us from looking around without judgement, frustration and panic. When we can cut through the negativity and hear what sounds are nearby, we are more open to the natural flow of energy all around. In our modern and digital age, it is of course harder for us to be connected with nature. We aren't out foraging for food with a great understanding of the seasons. We have watches to know the time, and don't have to only rely on the placement of the sun in the sky. We aren't having to walk miles through differing terrain to get places. We work at a speed and with that comes a price. We have

sped up so much of life that we miss out on stuff.

I don't know about you but when I'm in nature, I instantly notice how much less fizz and noise there is in my head. I take the time to look around and experience, rather than constantly judging and deciphering or taking a bloody photo for Instagram.

Mini Holidays

Being in the moment isn't always easy but it is a fast track to stopping the constant Chatter from taking over. If we are truly in the NOW, we can only really observe and experience as there is no room or time to explore the obstacles of the past or the unknown of the future – triggers for our negative voices. Our ancestors will have had to have lived in the moment, as survival was a much more urgent thought than it is today for most of us, whereas we think years ahead of where we are stood today and get dragged back to years gone by as we let our brains fill up with worry and regret. Because of how quickly we move in this day and age, we are constantly planning ahead. What might we wear to the pub with our mates next Saturday night? (Or in my case, which pair of pjs might I wear while watching a movie on the sofa?) What could we achieve at work in the coming year? What new thing are we saving up for in the future? We give the NOW a lot less limelight as we usually believe things will be better in the future.

Being aware that this weird myth we have come to believe is untrue gives us the opportunity to just enjoy the bits of life we are living right NOW. Of course we can still plan and get excited for things on the horizon but we need some balance. If we remember that stressing about the past or worrying about the future brings up a lot of mental Chatter then we can clearly see the importance for some clarity and calm in the NOW.

Maybe as you relax into the now and notice what sounds and smells are in your vicinity (for me, it's the trickling of the water down the drainpipe that my stepdaughter has just let out of the bath and the rich scent of the coffee in my nearby cup), you'll experience a reduction in negative thought. A few straggly regular thoughts might try to edge their way in as you concern yourself with what you're going to cook for dinner or recall that you forgot to text someone back earlier, but if we can remember to let those thoughts appear and then float away again then we can start to see the importance of being in the now, where we might just find a big chunk of quiet.

In our busy lives, it can be very tricky to have large stretches of time like this and that's why, at my very beginner's level of effort, I think of these quiet moments as little treats. Mini holidays from the craziness of my usual mental Chatter. Glorious islands of nothingness among the chaos of constant thought. It often feels a little scary to me as my usual plate-spinning as a working mum feels like a hazardous and overly vigilant job. If I stop thinking about what is coming next, won't every plate smash to the ground? It feels like the clatter of a Greek dinner party is only moments away if I take my eye off the ball. Yet I also know that I need these moments of quiet to be an efficient mum and worker. A brain that thinks constantly without break will of course run itself into the ground at some point and possibly make me even less efficient in the long run. Most of us need to think of these moments of quiet as less of a treat and more of an absolute necessity.

Awareness is otherwise known as the much awkwardly muttered and usually misunderstood word 'mindfulness', or 'awake-fullness', as my dear wise mate Zephyr Wildman likes to call it. When we take the time to be present, we can slow everything down and be aware of what is real and what is mind faff, and then we can silence the negative voices and not let them rule over our lives.

Write down all your future
worries and stresses of
the past in these bubbles.
Imagine them floating away
for now (these thoughts can
come back to you in a while
if you need them to).
Then just enjoy the
quiet in the NOW.

HELLO TO . . . GILES YEO

You may have noticed I have used the word 'gut' quite a few times already in this book. Many cultures believe that the gut is actually where it is at. It is another 'brain', if you will, guiding us and steering us to reach our full potential. It's no coincidence we use the phrases 'go with your gut' or 'gut feeling'.

I wanted to find out more about the much-neglected gut and how we should respect and honour its power and therefore learn how to harness its full capacity to guide us in life. If we can all listen to the gut a little more, the negative voices in our minds have to learn to take a back seat. I quizzed Giles Yeo, a neuroscientist specialising in gut-health, about the true power of the gut and how it works with the rest of our bodies.

F: Hi Giles! Thanks so much for talking to me. So, first up: do you think we underestimate how much our gut health has an impact on our generalmental health?

G: I do think we underestimate it in terms of our general well-being. How well we feel on any number of levels depends on our diets and on the quality of our diets as well. The gut communicates with the brain via hormones. And that has a very big role to play in the feelings of being full and of hunger as well. But what is not actually appreciated is how much the gut communicates with the brain. The gut is sometimes called the second brain because there are actually whole sheaths of 'neuronal' tissues, nerves and 'neurones' that surround it. So there is a huge amount of hardwired communication between the brain and the gut going on at any one time.

F: If we do have poor gut health, how can that have an impact on our brain?

G: That depends what you mean by poor gut health. Clearly, if you are having some acute gastrointestinal distress you'll be in pain and then that's a different kind of thing. Your gut is a huge organ – it's 21ft long, and so there is a lot of gut to be unwell. If you're feeling unwell in the gut you don't feel like eating properly, and if you don't eat properly, mentally you're just going nowhere. But ultimately it depends what is specifically wrong – whether or not it's an acute problem or a chronic problem, whether you're talking about stress, ulcers, inability to digest food etc. Each scenario has different outcomes on the body and the mind.

F: If there are raised levels of stress or anxiety, does that impact hormone levels that affect gut health?

G: I won't pretend to be an expert on that front, but I think the answer's going to be yes. When your cortisol stress hormone level goes up, your brain has to decide: what am I going to do with this stress and how am I going to respond to it? And I think one of the outputs is likely to go via the gut. And the interesting thing is we behave differently around chronic stress: some people eat more, some people eat less, some people eat more crap, some people feel they need to go exercise instead, and yet it's all based on this one same hormone. It's exactly the same hormone yet all of us have different strategies to solve it, and depending on what we choose to do or eat when we are stressed, that of course can influence our gut health and our overall health.

F: If you're stressed and you reach for something high in processed sugar, could that have a detrimental effect on your gut health?

G: If you have too much of it, yes. I know I personally need to stop that! But if you have one thing that's high in sugar, it's going to be absorbed before it does any damage to your gut at all. It's more of a problem if we end up eating less of a nutrient we really need, such as fibre. Very infrequently if we are stressed do we reach for celery – essentially if you're eating more bad stuff you'll be eating less good stuff, and that's actually what causes a drop in gut health.

F: What constitutes good gut health?

G: It depends on how you're measuring it. The best marker of good gut health is how regular you are. If you eat food and at a regular interval it comes out the other side in a compact solid form, then that's going to be good gut health in one way. There's another way of actually looking at it: how is your microbiome looking? The more varied the type of bugs we have in our guts, the better gut health we tend to have.

F: How would you advise someone to achieve good gut health?

G: It's the most boring answer in the world, but eating a well-balanced diet with enough fibre is the answer.

F: When we say 'go with your gut' is that because the gut is actually helping us decipher and problem-solve?

G: No, it's your brain that's going to help you do the problem-solving! However, as I've said above, because your gut is so tightly packed in with nerves, there is an output from your brain to your gut that you can feel. So if you're nervous and you have a sensation that you need to run to the loo, that's because your brain is communicating with your gut. There are no pain receptors in the brain, whereas there are plenty of receptors and signals that we can sense from the gut – any feelings associated with your gut are actually coming directly from the brain.

F: Last question: our brains constantly try and override our gut decisions. How do we start to root back to listening to our guts?

G: Oh, I don't know if that's true. I think your gut makes no decisions. Imagine it like this – if you've seen *Despicable Me* you'll know Gru instructs the Minions, who are all working underneath him yet for him. Your brain is Gru, your gut is the Minions. So in effect, whilst we call them 'gut decisions' or 'gut feelings', what you actually need to do is listen to your brain.

Tapping into our Guts

Having spoken with Giles, I feel I need to get to know my own gut on a more personal level. I love understanding how the body works and how the physical and mental have to work in tandem to create balance in life. As Giles said, if we keep our guts healthy we will have an all-round better state of well-being, which must equate to more clarity and better decision-making. If our bodies feel vibrant and in balance we have less mental stress and pain, so hopefully a little more quiet in the brain department too. I know it's not always easy as many out there suffer with physical ailments even though they care greatly for their bodies, but if you do feel there is room for diet improvement, why not give it a go?

When we say 'go with your gut' it isn't physically our guts making a call but instead an intuition or deep knowing that we follow before the pros and cons questions kick in. It is similar to when we say we love with our hearts: those feelings will likewise come from the brain, but the heart is the body part we associate with those feelings. Perhaps we use the word 'gut' in reference to a sort of inner knowledge because, as Giles says, it communicates with the brain so much and is able to register feelings in a different way. If someone asks us if we want to move to another country with them there will be an initial feeling. It could be of excitement or of complete dread but whatever the feeling, those first few moments of reacting will be purely felt rather than laced with words, and often that feeling is within the pits of our stomachs. Our 'gut' instinct. The feeling before our brain Chatter sparks up to usually confuse the hell out of us. Getting some confidence around following those feelings is something I'm constantly striving for and perhaps we can learn to trust it a little more together as we work through this book.

First Step: Done

Quiet Observation to me is a combination of noticing the triggers for our own inner dialogue. This might be certain people in our lives, fears and phobias or the unknown in life, and what the inner Chatter sounds like. Once we recognise what those triggers are we have a little more control over how the Chatter plays out. We already know that a potentially nerve-wracking situation could spark up our Inner Naysayer so we are one step ahead of the game. We know what to expect. We also know what those voices sound like so they instantly have less power and punch. We know every possible acerbic phrase or slur that could come into play so we can be a little more ready to combat them by inserting some positive phrasing, following our gut instinct or just settling into some quiet. Recognising what causes our brain Chatter to start spouting off is half the battle so get ready to observe yourself like you are your own science experiment and make friends with the plethora of voices you may experience. Then we can work on the next step – NOT taking them all so seriously.

If I stop and recognise my thought patterns I can make a choice as to whether I am ruled by them or not.

2

Quiet Confidence

When I look at my own melting pot of inner voices which make up the confusing sound wall of negative Chatter I experience daily, I think my confidence is the part of me that is affected the most. I'm sure if asked most of you would come to the same conclusion. Some of the negative voices are louder than others and seem to have more power over me, but all in all my confidence is still the part of me that suffers most. Negative Chatter seems to feed off low confidence and so it becomes a vicious circle of doom. So, in this chapter, I'll be looking at how we inflate our inner confidence and shut down the Chatter that tells us 'we can't'. This chapter is all about 'WE CAN!'

The Confidence Bashers

The voices that affect my self-esteem the most are the 'Naysayer' and the 'Evil One'.

Let's start with the Naysayer, who sounds pathetic from the get-go right? The voice that would rather stoop its shoulders and slump around in ill-fitting baggy clothing than stand spine straight with head held high to try again or overcome mishaps. This voice is heavy and knows how to push my buttons. It knows my weak spots, so lurks around in those shady corners waiting for an opportunity. It's a part of us that is a little fed up and hasn't the energy to turn the sour into sweet or the lacklustre into excitement. It's a part of us that is jaded and lethargic and generally can't be arsed to try.

Now, I may look confident to you. Perhaps you have seen me on TV or heard my podcasts and assume I am confident to the core. Well – I'm not. I will happily break that myth by spilling out some of my most vulnerable memories. I can be confident and content and sometimes even confident and a little feisty, but I can also be the absolute opposite due to that negative Chatter in my head.

The Naysayer Voice doesn't just wait for the moments that are big and important, it seizes any given opportunity to overshadow self-belief

or confidence. Some days, I wake up feeling rather brilliant and bounce into my local café with big smiles and big chat. I'm up for a conflab with other friendly locals about the weather or what Meghan Markle wore the day before. There might not be any particular reason why I'm feeling positive and confident that day, it's just a good one and I'll roll with it. On a not so good and bouncy day, I'll be much more aware of the Naysayer Voice telling me that I need to dress low key, keep my head down and be monosyllabic at the best. This might be down to tiredness, or stress I'm experiencing but whatever the reason it'll have a firm grip on my confidence and how I present myself that day.

The Power of Passion

As well as the small and sometimes insignificant in life, confidence is, of course, needed for the juicy stuff: making changes, moving forward and trying new things. Sometimes confidence arrives on the scene without warning and that is a rather delicious and much-needed boost.

When we fall in love, we often feel naturally fortified with a new inexplicable confidence. When I met my husband, I definitely felt like this and lapped it up big time. I wore clothes I normally felt too dressy in and walked with hair swishing like Beyoncé mid-dance routine. Bloody brilliant. I laugh/smile when I look back on those first few love-filled weeks. Not many voices were present in my head at that point either. Love makes you feel powerful enough to tell your negative thoughts to fuck right off so you can experience the intoxicating and insanely spontaneous qualities of it all. Stay out until 4 a.m. drinking gin on a work night, you say? Well, why the hell not? Dress up on a Tuesday in clothes you haven't worn in years, I hear you cry? Why bloody NOT! Move to another country where I know no one, you say? Well, why not? (I didn't actually do this one but it's certainly a well-told story elsewhere.)

New love makes us do the craziest most extreme things because there is no room for negative Chatter due to love's big, bouncy, mouth-watering size. It's too ginormous and too all-consuming. Chatter doesn't stand a chance. This new buzzy love has an expiry date of course, and when it begins to dissipate can leave a rather level-headed, grounded and equally gorgeous love. The head Chatter usually starts to return at this point as we settle in to a new rhythm and perhaps that is what makes brand-new love so intoxicating.

I have felt this love and lack of head Chatter with new friends, jobs and places as of course it is not exclusive to people. It might be a new hobby we have stumbled upon that seems to take up so much of our headspace or a new city or country visited. We focus much more on the

feelings that are present than the constant dialogue in our heads. The power of positivity. When we are in the flow of love, creativity, newness or learning, we forget about all of the negative Chatter and concentrate on the good stuff. With this usually comes an underlying confidence to do more of the above.

My confidence has waxed and waned over the years but definitely revved up a notch when I met my dear hub, Jesse. At this point I was 29 and very disheartened by relationships. I was genuinely considering adoption and a life where I relied on no other. Of course, that is exactly when Jesse rocked up.

Prior to this, I entered most relationships in life assuming that I was always in the wrong and that I should feel lucky to be with someone. ZERO confidence present. My fear of losing a partner, due to the undesirability the mental Chatter was affirming, was huge. The Chatter would tell me regularly that I was not as smart as I should be or was perhaps dressing in too quirky a manner to be desirable. I stunted my own emotional growth in these times and didn't shine my inner light as brightly as I feel I'm now able to. We all have a strong inner light that is so easily and instantly extinguished when our negative Chatter rises up. It can be as quick as the flick of a light switch. No dimmer switch on this one. The Naysayer Voice sparks up – and off that light goes.

I think this display of self-doubt is prevalent in most

Write down any activities that you love or have brought you joy in the hearts. Do you recall the feeling of a little more quiet in those times? Are you doing them enough?

twenty-somethings' lives. We are, at this point, still finding our feet in the big wide world and don't always have the confidence to speak up and say our bit. Maybe this is exactly as it should be so that we stumble, make mistakes and then learn to pick ourselves up and turn down new roads. It can be an adventurous decade where we perhaps travel after education, find new love and settle down for the first time, start families, new careers or move away from where we grew up. It's usually a time of great change – a state our negative voices like. So many corners and loose ends for negativity to grab hold of. So much newness for the Chatter to narrate. So many stumbling blocks that the Chatter can take ownership of. I'm not saying that after this decade these voices all naturally fade away – along with the smell of cheap cider and fag ends (that was my twenties anyway) – to be replaced with fragrant notes of laundered clothing and a brain with no Chatter. No – the subsequent decades can be equally as perplexing, but perhaps there is a little more awareness of one's self and an inch more confidence thrown into the mix due to the life lived beforehand. After adolescence and the growth we experience in our twenties, it is possible for us to become more aware of the negative voices we hear and the potholes in life that trigger them.

Learning Confidence

I like to personally call my twenties 'a very fun shit show'. Don't get me wrong, there were many, MANY fun times: a lot of laughter, a fortunate lack of ill health, a lot of great friends, travel and adventure. This decade also presented learning in the form of failure, hurt and chaos. From these trickier times came a lot of opportunities to learn. I guess this is another excellent reason for us all to strive to silence a lot of the Chatter we hear. If we can get through tough times and not let the Chatter talk us out of trying again then we have the opportunity to learn. We can find the lessons among the shit and toe-curling memories and try something new or see things in a new light. Knowing this allows us to be bolder – making mistakes isn't so bad after all. I have only learned this lesson by fucking up big time. By allowing others to treat me badly, by not having my say, by not being 100 per cent authentic to what I believe and who I am and by giving way too much of a toss about what others thought of me.

Wanna hear some of the things I've learned over the years so you can feel better about your own mistakes/can see how my confidence has grown because of them? Go on then . . .

Lesson number 1

If someone is being a twat to you, you usually don't deserve it. I naturally assumed during this decade that anyone that was mean, overpowering or talked down to me was 100 per cent right and I was uneducated in areas and always wrong. Even though I know I have always had a rather good gut instinct and understanding of emotional intelligence, I would let the internal Chatter tell me otherwise. The Inner Critic would agree with those around me and talk down to me so I either became mute or nodded nicely. FUCK THAT!

These days, if I disagree with what someone is saying or how someone is acting, I speak up. This doesn't mean I do it from a place of anger (okay, sometimes I do) but rather from a place where I deeply believe injustice is afoot. I am able to stamp on the fire that has been started by a match struck by the Naysayer and can open my mouth and let the truth spill out. I can sniff injustice and ego out so much more easily than I could in my twenties. My confidence in this department has most definitely grown over time. Time and practice. The practice bit is important as I do believe life experience gives us an ability to read signs and then act accordingly and appropriately. The Naysayer Voice may still have a hold on me in some of life's more fragile situations, but I do feel the grip loosening somewhat as time passes.

Lesson number 2

You don't have to be out at a party or associated with a particular group of people to feel you fit in to society. I used to feel I had to be part of a gang, whether I actually liked them or not, to be of any worth. My own unique qualities, good and bad, weren't visible enough to me to feel they had any value. I felt others would assume I was too boring, or not interesting enough to be liked. The Inner Critic would vehemently fortify this worry by telling me that people were not listening to me when I spoke and thought of me as rather dull. Being part of a group to simply be at a party, bustling with the energy of the room, made me feel like I was, by osmosis, more interesting.

Again, SOD THAT!

When I am in bed reading my book at 9 p.m. on a Friday night I now, in my mid-to-late thirties, feel enough. I can quash the Inner Critic and its whining tones and feel a contentment I couldn't grasp in my twenties. This voice may try and get in cahoots with its dear old friend, the FOMO Voice, to tell me I'm boring and missing out on so much fun, but I know from life experience that the quiet and peace I feel when relaxing at home is much more potent than anything else out there. I do still go out, but for different reasons. I don't go to feel part of something, to boost my own confidence, as I already feel that within the unit of my family and with the deep-rooted friendships and connections I've made with people over my lifetime. It's all about doing what makes YOU feel right, whether that's cuddling with a hot water bottle on a solo night of Netflix consumption or out partying until 4 a.m. with your best mates.

Lesson number 3

Confidence isn't the loudest person in the room. I used to lust after those I worked with and socialised with who seemed so naturally comfortable shouting from the rafters. Again you may assume that when I'm out with friends or at a party that I might be the one dancing on tables to Taylor Swift with a loud hailer in hand. I've never really been the type. There may have been a few incidents where one too many gins made me believe I could perform a rather soaring karaoke version of Adele (NEVER choose an Adele song at karaoke), or even crowd surf (don't get too excited, it was a Hanson concert circa 2008), but only very rarely. I've always preferred deep conversation, connection and observation but still believed that my lack of confidence in areas was holding me back from being the life and soul of the party. The Chatter would tell me that these louder, bolder characters I had witnessed had life sorted and must feel amazing inside. I believed this brain Chatter and its twisted words which would often make me sink deeper into my own skin and self-doubt – or at least a little closer to the bar for another drink to mute this doubt.

I have been fortunate to interview so many interesting characters over the years and the lesson I've learned from that experience is that it is more often than not the quietest, calmest types who hold a lust-worthy inner confidence. The louder types are often hiding behind a joke or perhaps a tell-all story as they are trying to shout down their own Inner Critic.

These days I love to talk with all manner of characters and enjoy reading between the lines as I can clearly see those who are comfortable in their own skin and those who might look like they are, but perhaps aren't at all. Once we know and understand our own Inner Naysayer and Critic, we can see the same in other people with much more clarity. A breakthrough moment, for sure.

If you are in your twenties reading this part of the book, I hope you don't feel patronised or talked down to as I'm honing in on what I personally learned. You may have learned all of this in your teens, or are learning it and understanding it right now, in which case you're getting to grips with it a lot sooner than I did! Everyone's timeline and path taken is different and will present us with bespoke lessons in life and confidence.

The Mother of All Inner Critics

At this point in life my Naysayer has crept into the parenting part. It will tell me that I'm not a good enough mum. I should encourage the kids to eat more adventurous food. I should be more fun even when I've barely slept the night before. I should get them out of the bad habits I've allowed them to create, like eating toast in my bed and watching TV when they are eating. I waste hours worrying and ruminating as this Chatter takes over. Now, going back to our glorious gut and that instinct that goes beyond reason or calculation: that gut of mine fires up a feeling deep within me that 'knows' that I am enough. It knows that my children have bucketloads of love delivered to them daily and that I would do anything for them. I have to apply some effort, replace those habitual negative thought patters with some positive acknowledgements and give myself a blinking break. Not always easy but, again, it's all down to practice.

We only jump straight for those negative thoughts because we are used to doing so. Perhaps pick one simple sentence you can apply to a plethora of situations and jump to that instead of the negative. 'I AM ENOUGH' usually does the trick for me. I can run that sentence over

What does your Inner Naysayer usually tell you? Write down three examples below and then next to each of those sentences write a new positive spin on it. So, for example, 'I'm rubbish at relationships' might become 'I'm worthy of meeting someone amazing'.

Each time you hear that particular sentence rear up, replace it with the new phrase.

Negative thoughts	Positive thoughts

and over in my head and it acts as a bit of a dam for all the negativity trying to break through. It's a small sentence that leads to a big chunk of quiet.

Accepting Ourselves

The other voice that affects my confidence on a subterranean level is the Evil One. This voice isn't necessarily articulate in any way. It only needs a few words and a scrap of a narrative to bring me down. Plainly speaking, it calls me a piece of shit. Failure will usually be the catalyst for this voice to rear its monstrous head. It is an entirely unnecessary and irrational voice but I'm sure one we have all dealt with in times of stress. I have had so many interesting conversations with brilliant women in my life who have admitted to self-loathing, all spurred on by this mental Chatter. Women who look robust and glowing from the outside. Women who hold a seat of power in their field of work or within a community. Women who look jaw-dropping in their splendour. Many have felt the wrath of this confidence-sapping internal voice. So just know when you next feel beaten down by your own Chatter, you are not alone in the slightest – in fact, I'd go as far as saying I'm pretty sure we are all massively in the majority.

So few escape this sort of Chatter.

My own self-loathing luckily isn't omnipresent, as again with age I have learned about self-love, something I'll look at in depth in the next chapter. I have come to my own conclusion that it is entirely necessary and conducive to live a contented life. I must personally buck against what has been presented to me growing up in Britain and must remember that being stoic and suppressed aren't always the best ways. I know that self-love has to come from accepting my faults, owning my mistakes and knowing I have risen from pains and tough times before. I can now usually (maybe less so on a bad day) look at myself squarely in the mirror and know that, over the years, I have been brilliant, careless, loving, selfish, grounded, irrational, giving and shut off and that is all okay. I am human and fallible, yet willing to acknowledge all that I am. Self-love isn't about ignoring the bad bits or pretending we have never fucked up, it's about accepting it all and still liking yourself.

Liking ourselves is an idea that's much easier to digest than suggesting that we actually 'love ourselves'. That feels too self-indulgent or egotistically sybaritic to admit. It shouldn't be, but we have been socially conditioned to believe so. We would be deemed big-headed or full of ourselves if we do it, but as I said I don't believe self-love is all about looking at the best bits like we've been edited down into an X-factor-style montage; it's about seeing ourselves as a whole and accepting what that looks like.

What do you see when
you look in the mirror?
Write a description or
draw a picture here.

The Slippery Slope of Self-Loathing

So back to the other side of the coin: self-loathing. Why on earth do we put ourselves through such self-torture? Pointless, time-wasting – perhaps even more self-indulgent than completely loving oneself. Complete and utter sabotage. I self-loathe when something goes wrong at work. The negative Chatter ignores the basics – that I have made a mistake and learned from it – and shortcuts to telling me that I am a useless piece of shit. Straight for the jugular. No long windy road of rumination to end up there. Straight to 'I am a piece of shit', delivered on a platter by the Evil Voice within. This voice points out how everyone else is doing so well and that I am doomed and have been tarnished with a thick tar-like marking that notifies people that I am useless.

I have, like most people, cocked up at work. Occasionally due to a lack of understanding or time applied, but also as a result of just pure bad luck or misfortune. My Evil Voice doesn't care how I got myself into such a pickle as it will pipe up regardless. I have had moments where others have felt the need to poke fun at my mistakes: a stumbled word on the radio, a mispronounced name on live TV, and this has only heightened my feeling of utter worthlessness. The Evil One loves having mates along for the ride so along comes The Voice of Others, and I start to believe every word said and take complete ownership of those comments. At its worst, I have had this voice ringing in my ear for a good few months. Perhaps longer, as it tailed off to make way for other slightly less irritating inner dialogues, but nonetheless, it's a long, compacted and torturous time of self-loathing.

It is, of course, very hard to be confident in what you're doing when you start to believe that negative Chatter. When those words become who you are rather than what you are thinking, it can take a turn for the worse. I have definitely had several moments where my confidence has been torn to shreds and I have had trouble stringing a sentence together. I have only been able to dig myself out of these holes with loved ones around me. Perhaps a catch-22, as you don't feel you can be that close to others when you're feeling worthless, but it's imperative nonetheless. Human connection and another person's words spoken aloud do have the influence to overshadow our internal Chatter and demand its surrender, if we are willing to truly listen and try to change what we have begun to believe. I could write a list as long as this page with the names of people who have had this overriding impact on my life and will never stop thanking them or being there for them when they need a little of the same in their lives. Listening to someone else who is not put off by your misdemeanours and truly hearing their love can sometimes

Most of us need to work on accepting ourselves for who we are. So on the left-hand side of the person here, write down any bits of yourself – personality-, physically-, or emotionally-based – that you don't like. Then on the opposite side, dig deep and write down the same number of things that you DO like about yourself. Then write in the box below – with as much confidence as you can muster –
'ALL OF THIS IS ME, AND THAT IS OKAY.'

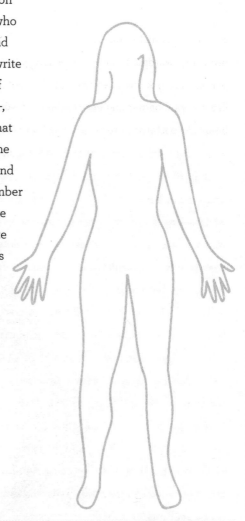

be enough to make you start hearing their words more loudly than your own. Their words are really only tapping into the truth and also what you perhaps really know deep down in that gut. Sometimes we all have to listen a little harder and believe the kind words spoken to us so we can break the patterns of self-loathing and find a little quiet.

HELLO TO . . . BRYONY GORDON

I recently interviewed my great mate, journalist and author Bryony Gordon, for my podcast series, *Happy Place*. If you have read Bryony's books or listened to her speak, you'll know how honesty spills out of her like lava from a volcano. She cannot NOT tell the truth. She says it how it is and has told her story so eloquently and beautifully, warts and all. I so massively admire her storytelling and how it has helped others, and also her personal acceptance of all that has been and currently is. I am on a desperate quest to find out how she has reached that sweet spot of acceptance. If you follow Bryony on Instagram, you'll know that her honesty and self-confidence is displayed perfectly in her authentic life shots. One day, she may have her beautifully bouncy bosom thrust towards her camera phone for all to see. Other days, she may be in her underwear running a marathon. This is a particular area of confidence I think we all lack as women. Bryony's confidence spans her ability to step out of her comfort zone with big challenges, how she shares her own story and her acceptance of what life has thrown her way.

The physical side of things really interests me as it seems like such a big problem for a lot of us. We never feel like we are physically quite enough. We are too narrow-hipped, too squidgy round the tummy, too short in the leg, too long in the torso, too crooked in the nose, too small in the eyes, too thick in the arms, too small round the bottom. We have been presented an ideal of what a woman should be for so many years that it seems almost genetically ingrained into our DNA that we will never look quite right. Luckily, as time passes, we are seeing so many more points on the spectrum of beauty. OF COURSE, we all know that beauty is not one thing. Beauty IS, I believe, that inner confidence and lack of inhibition shining outwards and is a diverse and non-specific quantity of inexplicable light; yet, most of us still feel we don't match up.

When I last spoke to Bryony I quizzed her on this issue as I often feel like I'm not keen on how I look. It is usually more a state of mind, but I end up pinning it on to how I look that day. I wanted to understand the alchemy of Bryony's new-found body confidence. Luckily, dear BG was up for me quizzing her further here in this book to help spread her all-round joy and delicious vivacity for life as well as her tricks and tips for combating that confidence-zapping Chatter.

F: First up, I'm in total awe of you running two marathons, not least because you did the second in your underwear. Tell me about the reception you got on that hot April day.

B: The reception was INCREDIBLE. People we didn't know had made banners for us. But it was also quite poignant, because there were women running up to us telling us how ashamed they were of their bodies – their bodies that they were running a marathon with! I realised then the extent of self-loathing, and how it is etched into our national psyche.

F: Were you surprised as to how many you inspired?

B: I am always surprised that I have inspired anyone, because like everyone else I suffer from imposter syndrome and feel like a bit (a lot) of an idiot most of the time. But I am honest about it, and maybe that is what resonates with people.

F: So many women have body issues or self-loathe due to how they look. Our mental Chatter goes into overdrive on this one. How have your feelings towards your body changed over the years?

B: Well for a start I try and be kind to my body and look after it. For a long time I treated it appallingly and it's kind of a miracle I am alive. I drank too much, took drugs, had bulimia, didn't sleep. It was as if I was trying to punish myself for just existing. I have had to change that, because I knew if I carried on I would probably die. Life is too short. I want to squeeze out every precious moment of it.

F: We are very much told by the media and society that women should look and act a certain way which seems rather archaic in this day and age. How do you go against this and install self-acceptance and a positive outlook on how you look and feel?

B: Well, at least once a week I like to post a picture of myself on

Instagram as I actually am, no filters, in my underwear, because I think it's important to show things as they are, lumps, bumps, textures and all. It feels kind of empowering.

F: Do you think most of us get better with this one with age?
B: I think that as I've got older and had a daughter of my own, I've become more conscious of how I want her to grow up, and that encourages me to be better with it! I don't want her growing up with the self-loathing I did.

F: When your inner Chatter tells you to not bother going for a run how do you tell it to shut up?

B: I remember that my brain doesn't always want the best for me, and that while I never actually want to go for a run, I've never, ever regretted going for one!

Taking a Compliment

When somebody compliments you on your outfit when you get to work, or a friend praises you for such a beautifully cooked meal, is your response one of self-deprecation? Mine is usually along the lines of 'oh, this old thing, I think I look a bit of a mess actually' or 'well, it's only a quick rushed something I knocked up'. It takes true confidence to accept a compliment and not feel awkward about it.

Our negative mind Chatter may self-analyse after we have experienced a moment like this, with perhaps the Inner Critic Voice popping up to tell you that you shouldn't just take compliments willy-nilly as the other person involved will just think you are arrogant and a bit of a twat. Firstly, that is not true and, secondly, the other person involved is very rarely thinking about you post-conversation at all.

Most of us walk around worrying and replaying moments in our heads due to that Inner Critic voice. We may repeat conversations verbatim wondering how we came across, berate ourselves for having not stood up for ourselves more or for saying something that could appear big-headed. This is where we have to work back to the 'feelings' around a conversation rather than the words spoken. If we tap into those feelings, the words around the situation start to fade and we can reach a little quiet. We stop worrying if we have come across badly or if our words were taken out of context as we can find some quiet in knowing how we felt in that very moment. This is how we can find our confidence and stop worrying about every word uttered.

When you were speaking those words, or accepting that compliment, did you feel like you were coming from a place of arrogance or from a place of inner confidence? The other person involved will more than likely have picked up on your energy around those words rather than the words themselves, so tell your Inner Critic to remember this and to stop planting questions and concerns in your head. If you know you are useless at accepting compliments, why not try this out next time: say 'thank you' and smile without a caveat. Then give a compliment back to keep those good vibes rolling.

It is perhaps hard for us to find that sweet spot that sits somewhere in between celebrating our successes and believing our own hype. Our mind Chatter gets very confused and loud in these moments. True confidence untinged by ego will be the magic that allows us to look back at life's milestones or successful moments without allowing it to define us to the core. It goes back to looking at ourselves fully. The good bits and the tough bits and remembering we are all of it. Can you find the quiet in amongst it all, no matter what your story is? That's what I am currently trying to do. I am taking a more realistic look at myself and

I'm getting more confident in who that person is. I am the successes and failures, the fast and the slow, the determined and the lazy. And that is okay.

Confidence is the armour which allows us to speak freely without worrying what others think. How much time have we all wasted wondering what others think of us? Did our best friend think we were being selfish when we didn't offer to pay for dinner last week? Did our new love interest find us boring when we were reminiscing about a time that they didn't experience? Did the interviewer for a new job think we came across uneducated and lacking in skill? True confidence allows us to just be, well . . . us, and speak the words that feel right.

I have had many a sleepless night, and I mean that literally and not figuratively, where the Inner Critic has had me going over conversations again and again. Perhaps I asked someone a question out of pure intrigue but now the mental Chatter is telling me that it will have been taken as intrusive and out of line. The Inner Critic loves to analyse the most intricate of moments and blow them up like a rising hot air balloon. The size of these tiny moments becomes so inflated that we become blind to what was really going on. Maybe those concerns were true but if we know that we asked that question of our friend from a good place, reminisced in a joyful and fun way and did our best in the job interview, then what does it matter? We are never going to 100 per cent please everyone and having confidence means accepting that. Yet, of course, there are a plethora of other outcomes that we are failing to see because the mind Chatter is so negative. Maybe the other person in question didn't find us boring, intrusive or lacking in skill when we were chatting to them. Maybe, just maybe, they thought we were great!

Our confidence cannot be infiltrated in a negative way by the Chatter if we really consider our good intent. Are we coming at a situation from a good place? A grounded place and a place of love? If so, then the words spoken are only a part of the story. We have all slipped up and said things that came out wrong or asked a question in a sloppy way even when the intent was good. If we know deep down that we meant no harm or malice and also can justify our beliefs, even if they differ to others', then our confidence can remain intact and we can find a little quiet among all of that bad brain Chatter.

I'm not good enough

you could have been better

I wouldn't have done that

I'm not sure about that

Please don't do that

you shouldn't do that

I don't understand you

What is wrong with you?

Be Angry but Be Reasonable

This isn't to say we can never get angry if it's justified. We should be passionate and vehement in our line of conversation as long as we still truly believe there is good reason for us to say such things. Maybe we feel riled when someone treats us unfairly, so we feel we must be honest and say how we feel. Confidence has to come into play for us to be able to be clear about our own boundaries and beliefs so that we are heard and understood – without being arseholes. If we have been clear and others still choose to overstep the mark or cause us pain, we have to find empathy deep down and then have the confidence to try and see why the other person is hurting and acting out. NOT EASY, but better than ranting and raving inside and letting those frustrations manifest physically in ill health or fatigue – a trigger for more negative Chatter.

Our Inner Critic might tell us we have no place to stand up and say our piece but that is only because it is scared of the outcome and wants us to feel smaller than we are. We are all going to enter into a certain level of conflict with others in life as it is impossible to be agreeable all of the time. The Angry Voice may want its way in this sort of situation too and these are the moments when I personally really need to find my quiet. Before I fire off a shitty email or get fired up and say something loaded, I need to take a minute. It could be a few seconds where I breathe before choosing to retort. Sometimes longer is needed, so I will walk away and get some fresh air, or sleep on a matter, before reeling off an angry rant. The quiet in these moments allows me to get some much-needed clarity and gives me the space to see why I have been so riled.

Sometimes I find that what I at first found annoying has actually aggravated a previous wound. It has picked at a scab that was still healing and has brought up emotions from something else. I wouldn't have detected such a thing if I had reacted in the moment. Time and some quiet is always needed. (By the way, there have been loads of moments where I have not found some quiet and have said some regrettable things to people who have annoyed me. You live and learn and all that!)

We are all so different and have varying ideas about the world. That doesn't mean we can't live in a cohesive way; we just need to find the confidence to either say our bit or find some peace in the fact that we are all so very different. (Or swear loudly in private/go to a kick-boxing class or do other anger-releasing activities!)

It can be hard to silence that Inner Critic, but we must try to let the words flow freely even if it leads to confrontation or disagreement. These are the times when new roads can be laid and new pathways to peace can be travelled. I know that when I get shouty or aggressive in

a situation, it isn't always because I believe there is huge injustice, it's because I know deep down there are other emotions afoot. I might feel threatened or scared or perhaps a little out of my depth.

Yet if I confidently feel my point is worth putting across in a situation where I feel well-informed and grounded, I can still say my bit and be heard, yet in a calm and less confrontational way. It can take a lot more confidence to speak with a calmer tone and not get too het up, and coming from that place usually requires hitting up some of that quiet we've been talking about. I say this from a very well-practised place. I have said so many things in the past that I might not today (some I still would, mind!) and have let my Chatter take over and manifest as actual words.

What I perhaps regret more than sloppily spoken words are those times when I failed to combat the Inner Critic voice and bit my tongue when I wish I had spoken up. I have let work colleagues take the reins when I felt I had more to offer. I have gone against what I believe is truly right as I was listening to that Inner Critic talk me down and I have built up tensions around these silences that have left me feeling depleted and tense.

On one such occasion, I was in a confrontation with someone who I found very tricky to talk with. This individual generally seemed unwilling to see outside of their world and was very shut off to new ideas.

During this heated discussion, I bit my tongue several times as the Inner Critic held me back. I left this conversation and immediately got a fever. The feelings of injustice and hurt were so huge that my body didn't know how to channel the energy as I hadn't set these feeling free with words. My skin bubbled with the frustration and felt hot to touch. My body ached with the need to set this emotion free. It was a real shock but a good moment to reflect on how powerful this sort of transaction can be.

Knowing how to Behave

When we are faced with confrontation or differing opinions, we mustn't confuse confidence with anger or greed. We can hold our own, have an opinion but we can do it without stamping our feet and screaming the house down. We mustn't let the Chatter tell us that we have to win, yet neither should we allow it to tell us to keep mute. I guess the only way I have been able to silence these voices, or at least acknowledge them and then move forward, is to root back to the feelings afoot. If I know what I want to say will do some good or at least allow me to express myself clearly then I can open my mouth and say what is needed without losing control. It's one I try to practise when the opportunities arise. I almost dare myself to say my bit. I may hear the Inner Critic pop up and tell me to keep my mouth shut as I don't deserve a say, but I will then challenge it with a personal dare. I think of it as a chance to be courageous and experience the new. What would happen if I spoke the truth? Would it really be so bad? The worst that could happen is that this person takes offence, but if I truly believe in what needs to be said, then surely it would be worth it to reduce the chances of me harbouring resentment in the future?

Don't Stick

Inner negativity may also be to blame for holding us back within society, our friendship or work circles. Have you decided that you are the co-worker and not the boss? Has your negative Chatter told you that this is all you are capable of? Do you believe that you don't deserve to have good people in your life? Sometimes we feel our place within a community or social structure is set in stone and again a lack of confidence is enough to keep us there. When I was growing up with lofty dreams of working in TV, it didn't worry me that I had no connections to the industry at all. It didn't enter my head that it was far-fetched for a girl from the suburbs with a cockney lilt and fringe cut with kitchen scissors to work in such a glamorous business. I was nicely naive and ready for whatever was thrown my way.

After the door to the TV world opened, I started to be pulled towards listening to the Chatter. Did I really fit in? Am I worthy of working with other people more established on the TV? Do I belong at all? Over the last 21 years of my career, I have waxed and waned as to how much I let this Chatter take over the show. At times, I have felt confident in this space and have neglected this non-stop Chatter, yet at others, usually after failures or mishaps, I have very much believed every word I hear in my head. After certain failures I capped my growth and believed that I didn't fit into the industry like everyone around me. I didn't have the right qualities or thick skin to continue working at the speed I had. There have been moments where I have stunted my own growth as I listened to the voices within rather than lurching forward to the places I truly felt I could reach. Remembering that the positions we hold within family set-ups, the workplace and in society are malleable, is freeing in itself.

I think most of us know deep down if we've kept ourselves stuck in one place in life. This may be a weak spot that we can instantly recognise. At work, in relationships, when change is afoot. Whatever it is for you it'll be a portion of your life that stands out because it feels tricky. If you look a little closer, can you see real reason, for why there is failure or lack of growth in that area? If you look even harder, can you see that the reason is that your mental Chatter is holding you back?

I have had very clear moments in my career where I could have sat and blamed a number of people for my lack of growth, but I knew deep down inside it was me. I was the one telling myself I wasn't good enough and was stopping myself doing certain things at work that I felt too scared to try. As mad and confusing as it might feel to make this self-discovery, it is also very liberating as we can then start to try and change the dialogue within. You literally have to force that change at first. Noticing those cycles of Chatter and key phrases we hear on repeat is the first hurdle and once we've recognised those we can start to either block them out or begin to replace those sentences with new phrases – positive ones. It might feel all a little choreographed at first but it's a good starting point. If your key phrase is 'I'm not good enough' put a ban on it in your head and then replace it with 'I am enough'. Even if you don't believe it at first, it might give you enough room to try something new!

If we don't feel anchored or focused on where we want to head in life it is easy to look around and envy what others have or compare ourselves to them negatively, but we all also have the choice to look around and be massively inspired. How many people can you think of in the public eye or in your life who have pushed through social barriers or expectations to do what they truly believed was right? I can instantly list up some marvellous mavericks and keep them in mind next time I need or want to feel inspired.

- My dear friend Kris Hallenga, who lives with stage 4 cancer but doesn't let it rule her. She lives life to the fullest and travels, inspires and helps others constantly.

- Poorna Bell, who has not allowed the tragic loss of her husband stop her from connecting with others or striving for contentment in life. She has not let this trauma hold her back or keep her from reaching her full potential.

- My friend Heidi Greensmith, who hasn't let the fact that she has five kids stop her freelance work as a writer and director. It may take some insane juggling and organisation, but she hasn't let the fact her family life is very busy stop her from following her artistic flow.

- Katie Piper, who turns everything she touches to gold. She inspires so many people and didn't let her terrible misfortune earlier on in life debilitate her. She speaks to thousands, shines brightly and makes many people very happy.

- My friend Gok Wan, who was told by society that he was different to those around him. He ended up using this to his advantage and became one of the most glorious advocates for inner beauty and acceptance.

Each one of these mavericks inspires me greatly, along with a massive list of others which could quite literally be a whole other book. From where I'm sitting, they all have confidence in common and own who they are. They have surfed over the rough and smooth in life by harnessing their inner light and by not letting the mental Chatter hold them back and that, to me, is massively inspiring.

Confidence: the Lion Tamer

As I mentioned above, the strange catch-22 is that while our mental Chatter can curb our confidence greatly, it seems to be our confidence that can tame the mental Chatter. So what can we do if we feel beaten down and lacking in confidence? I think it's a little alchemy that we all have to practise and work on. Something that incrementally strengthens and feels more natural as we scramble through life.

Part of it is learning to notice when those damning mental

catchphrases rear up. There will be key ones for us all that we hear the loudest, ones that are easy to spot. The next job is to try and apply some discipline so we feel more in control. I often feel like I have so little control over my thoughts and that is when I usually spiral and end up feeling terribly down. Discipline and practice at tuning the negative out, trying and then perhaps trying again and again, will eventually mean we are used to shutting out certain confidence-damaging Chatter.

The first point to consider is that we have a choice. Even when it doesn't feel like we do as we are trapped in mental negative patterns, there lies a choice. If we on one particular day feel up to it we can challenge our own chatter and dare ourselves to do something different. If we wouldn't normally go up to a stranger to comment on their nice slacks as we feel too shy, we can dare ourselves to give it a go. What is the worst that could happen? I dare myself to do stuff constantly as it seems like a fun way to override the Chatter. In my line of work, I have to approach strangers, ask people I don't know well difficult questions and talk aloud. A lot of this arrives in the form of a dare to rival my Chatter. It is something that gets easier over time.

I have practised being confident so when I need to it comes to me a little easier. Remembering to think about the worst-case scenario is weirdly important. Although that sounds like a negative thing to do, it actually allows us to see that most of our fears have no acute result in mind. When I was single, I would think to myself: what would happen if I approached that attractive person on the train platform and just said 'hi'? What is the worst-case scenario? That they grimace and walk off? Okay, that might be embarrassing for about five minutes, but then what?

The fear of embarrassment holds us back so much, but it rarely has any depth. It is an emotion we may feel for a short while and then it fades and usually becomes a pretty hilarious story for others to hear. I've felt embarrassment on so many occasions. I've tripped over in a pair of flip-flops on holiday while trying to impress a boy by the pool. I've snorted when laughing while interviewing famous faces. My elbow has slipped off many chair arm rests while earnestly listening to someone. I felt embarrassed and then what? Not a lot. Don't let possible embarrassment hold you back. Practise daring yourself to try something new and see what happens.

Another point to remember is that we are not alone. We may look at others who seem to have it all sussed and walk around with complete confidence. I'm not sure that person exists and if they do, they're probably not willing to look at any of their own misdemeanours in life, which isn't very healthy at all. We are all equally as scared of tripping up, looking like a fool and failing. I have been fortunate enough to interview some incredibly talented and high-achieving people over the years, more recently for my podcast, *Happy Place*, and each and every person has admitted that if they peel back the layers, there's a vulnerable and slightly scared person.

Beneath all the accolades, titles, wealth and popularity, we are all the same. Knowing that always makes me feel better when I feel lacking in a situation. Knowing most people feel this under all the bravado or exterior chat, gives me great comfort and allows me to make slighter braver leaps.

Fake it Till You Make it

If all of this seems like a massive struggle, you can always fake it until you make it. Go for physically challenging yourself to walk into a room with more vigour and punch. Head held high and hands out of pockets. I dare myself to find that stance if I'm feeling nervous and sometimes the inner confidence follows suit and I flummox my mind into a false state of confidence. It's brilliant how the body and mind work in tandem in this way. If your body is on board, sometimes your mind just about follows, therefore shutting out the Chatter. I had a brilliant conversation with a successful actress about this once. Obviously, her speciality involves moving and changing for each of the characters she's inhabited. She would often hunch over to appear sad and find the tears followed suit as her brain got on board quickly with what was happening physically. She would move her diaphragm up and down to simulate laughter or tears and find that her emotions would follow suit because her brain matched the movements. Maybe we can all use this as a little shortcut to confidence. Then with a little practice, we might start feeling it for real too!

If I remember that the Inner Chatter isn't based on fact, I can act from the gut with confidence.

3

Quiet Self-love

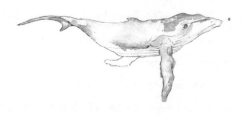

Surely the most potent of all remedies to our mental Chatter is self-love. If we can really get on board with this one we can use our self-love like weed killer, hosing down the voices until they recede back into the pockets of insecurity and fear where they came from. I have named this chapter 'Self-Love' purposely because I know deep down I have a problem with the term, and find my buttocks clenching whenever I even consider it. My husband will beg me to go and rest, take time out or simply give myself a break but I find it very hard.

The Inner Critic Voice doesn't think I deserve it. It will argue my gut feelings down and make me push on through – which of course is always more detrimental to everything I'm trying to achieve in the first place.

Shifting Our Focus

This is why self-love is so important, yet it is such a new and perhaps alien concept to so many of us Brits. We assume it's self-indulgent and unnecessary and put it to the bottom of the pile. It becomes one of those things we will get round to at some point, like turning the mattress over or clearing the loft out. It doesn't feel urgent or something we should bother with. We put family, work, social activities, plans for the future, shopping, pets, study . . . just about everything before it, yet if we aren't okay in ourselves, we can't actually do any of the aforementioned. So, why don't we put more focus on it?

Society doesn't always support the notion of self-love either as we are subliminally or sometimes very overtly fed information that we are not quite enough or perhaps need something or someone to feel full, whole and okay. As much as I love social media, it can make us feel empty and lacking when we have spent thirty minutes scrolling through the toned and tanned bodies of influencers' feeds we'll never meet. Then there's advertising, which is often presented in a way that makes us feel like we might just feel a little more complete if we purchase that new pair of shoes. As much as I love shoes and how transformative fashion

and beauty products can be I know deep down they are not going to 'fix me'. The whole point is I don't need fixing in the first place. I will always have my strengths and my weaknesses and that's okay. The only thing that can really remedy any inner and unwanted pain, tough memories or self-sabotage is some SELF-LOVE. EEEEK, it even makes my toes curl to write that yet I know it to be true. So, let's get stuck in to getting used to floating this notion about and feeling jolly well deserving and okay with it.

Accepting Our 'Failures'

Before we get to the actual 'love' bit, first we must understand the absolute opposite in order to conquer it. As I talked about in the previous chapter, not many of us will have gotten away scot-free without a little self-loathing along the way. Some deal with it on a daily basis. Some of us will beat ourselves up every time we fail. Some of us will curse ourselves in the mirror each morning for not looking a certain way. Some of us will pick apart each word we have spoken that week and feel full to the brim of regret. We dart in-and-out of the shadows, as any moment of self-reflection could send us running back into the darkness where we reprimand ourselves and only focus on the perceived negative.

Can you think of one recurring situation or person who makes you self-loathe? Is there a continuing altercation that weaves in and out of months of the year, softening and then peaking and each time sending you into a specific meltdown? Do you react by feeling your bespoke weaknesses heighten and engulf you? Do you only remember the times when you have failed and feel defined by them and chained to them?

Let's call them triggers; catalysts that could be small in size but always warrant the same reaction from us. I have a ton of these and I'm a typical Virgo in the fact that I like to stick to a pattern, so I find myself in the same hole without having learned from the previous experiences. The first important point is for us to notice these patterns. It is easy to point fingers at others but we have to take responsibility

and remember we have the power to change our repetitive reactions too. We must not let the mental Chatter drive us back down the same old, well-trodden roads if we know they don't work for us.

One way of doing this is to take a step back and look at how we view our own failures. I believe

that failure is incredibly important in life. No one enjoys failure but no one is exempt from it. It's inevitable in life and even those who look super shiny and 'perfect' will have experienced it in great doses. It's often the moment in which great success is inspired. Our own versions of success will differ in look, feel and size and it's imperative that we don't get caught up in other people's version of what this looks like. How we get there is much more important. It might be a lifelong expedition, but time is irrelevant. It's how we tread through the unknown terrain that counts. Failure is key in all of it. Without it we have no concept of true challenge, which is of course where we learn. Without it we have no opportunity to brush off the debris and rubble collected from catastrophic stumbles, dig our way out and walk again. Without it we have no chance of gaining strength and momentum and can easily become complacent. I know all of this deep down (in that glorious gut again) but so often allow the Chatter to talk all over this understanding.

I have failed many a time in my personal life and in my professional life and I'm almost at the point where I can be grateful for most of those potholes in the road. I can see the positives that have wildly grown from the damage. I can give thanks for the learning that sprouted from the cracks left wide open by mistakes made. I can use the strength that has amplified from moments of complete weakness. I can only view the aftermath of failure in a positive light if I allow myself that self-love.

It can only be in moments where I am softer and gentler with myself and stop the hateful talk within that I can recognise these failures as positives and remember that they do not make up the sum of all my parts.

The Bad Habits

Of course, after every single failure I have experienced in life I have fallen into line with a pattern of negative thinking that is very hard to break. The Chatter thrives in these moments. It suckles from the dripping sourness that oozes from every moment of failure and tries to take over our minds. I have berated myself for days, sometimes months, actually sometimes years, without remembering that I have to forgive myself at some point. We have to give ourselves a break and remember how normal and much needed life mistakes are.

On other occasions the mental Chatter starts up out of nowhere when everything is seemingly fine. It doesn't have to be a moment of mishap that ignites this negative mindset. The Chatter pops up to tell me I could have done better in moments that played out seemingly well. It picks holes in tightly woven moments of contentment. If there is a small gap these voices will creep in. Again, if we apply some self-care

Do you need to forgive yourself for a mistake or slip-up that constantly repeats in your head? Can you go back in time and mentally sit with that version of yourself and then forgive yourself? Write a list here of those moments and end your piece with 'I forgive me'. I hope this proves relieving for you in some way.

....

....

....

....

....

....

....

....

....

....

....

....

....

....

and love and give ourselves a break we can close those tiny gaps and stop the mental Chatter from seeping in. We can be kind to ourselves by remembering we did our best and that our intent was good so that the mental Chatter has little to grab hold of. We don't have to be 'perfect' (whatever the hell that is anyway) or on point every single day. We will have good days, bad days and 'whatever' days, which means our behaviour will run alongside that energy. On some days we will achieve greatly, on others not so much; that's just part of the human condition. All we can do is try and then take whatever result occurs and be kind to ourselves knowing we did our best on that particular day.

How to Talk to Yourself

Hands up who often talks to themselves like a piece of shit. (Me, me, me!!!!) I'm sure most of us have done when we have felt vulnerable or downtrodden. We talk to ourselves in a way we would not talk to others. We all, of course, have the propensity to be a bit of a wanker to those who irritate us but how we talk to ourselves is usually off-the-scale rude. I would never judge another's failure and then verbally rage at them. I would, instead, offer up comfort, solace and the opportunity to recover slowly. Why then are we so harsh on

In the speech bubbles below, write down some kind phrases you think you need to hear. Read them aloud and let these phrases override your negative Chatter.

ourselves? Why do we allow our negative Chatter to ignore common decency and take over the show?

The Evil Voice laps up any mistakes made with a salivating mouth and a book full of one liners. It grabs hold of comparison to others and notifies us that we are useless and tries to alienate us with shame. My Evil One not only tells me I'm a piece of shit in these moments, but also tries to persuade me to believe that everyone else thinks the same. My self-loathing has somehow leaked by osmosis into everyone else's subconscious. This is the part I find the trickiest. Often I can subdue and hide the self-loathing within my own head but when I start to believe the Evil One, then I almost forget how to interact with others without overthinking every word that comes out of my mouth. I approach each situation as if I'm talking to people who find me repulsive and somehow tarnished by my mistakes. I listen to this voice and my confidence subsides rather quickly, like water speeding down an open plughole.

I think most of us feel we are being judged by some unknown entity out there in the universe. Even if we're not religious, we feel something bigger than us is watching and perhaps holding up scores when we succeed or fail. The only one that is really judging us is ourselves. I think once we accept that, we can start to be kinder to ourselves and quieten those voices telling us otherwise. So, next time you hear negativity sparking up ready to take you down, take a moment to find a piece of quiet: stop and make a decision to not let that voice in. You may still recognise that thought and almost take notice of it, but remember to be kind to yourself.

We are not our mistakes, we are not our failures, we are all complex fallible creatures who need a bit of kindness. Introduce a kinder and softer approach in these moments and mentally talk to yourself like you would to a dear friend. We all then have the chance to recover properly from mistakes and slip-ups and without all of the horrid shame that often comes along for the ride.

I had a really interesting conversation with my friend Yvonne Williams, a counsellor, who told me to look back at my list of regrets in life and to be much kinder to the person I was then. To visualise travelling back in time to Fearne aged 24, picture taking her by the hand and telling her it's okay. There are things I know now that I didn't in my twenties, as those lessons hadn't yet been presented to me. We can begin to forgive ourselves and lessen the heat of those regrets and mistakes. We can recognise that while we might do things differently today, we needn't waste time and energy beating our former selves up just because the Chatter tells us to do so.

Time to get letter writing. Write to your younger self. Don't talk down to that version of yourself, just tell them it will all be okay. Forgive them and thank them for getting you the good stuff you have in your life today.

HELLO TO . . . DAWN O'PORTER

I could write a whole chapter on writer and presenter Dawn O'Porter alone. We began our friendship in unusual circumstances online. We were part of a large group email a mutual friend had sent out and then somehow started emailing each other privately about other matters. That then turned into a full-blown, five-year pen pal friendship! Pen pals! In our thirties! In the twenty-first century! Wonderfully archaic and lots of fun. I can't wax lyrical enough about how ace it is to have an online buddy who you've never met. Yes, that's right: we had NEVER met, yet spoke for five years about everything from breast-feeding to boxsets on a very regular basis.

During one of our lengthy emails reporting the ins and outs of our lives – mine in rainy Blighty, hers in dreamboat LA – she mentioned that she was over in the UK the following month, visiting family. An immediate date was set and the next thing I knew Dawn and her two beautiful boys were ringing the doorbell. Saying hi was weirdly normal. A stranger without the awkwardness and a hug that felt new yet very at ease. We rabbited away for a good couple of hours and picked up from where our last email had left off. A joyful day all round. Luckily meeting me in person didn't put off dear Dawn and we have continued to email ever since as she is now back in her new home of America.

Not only has she become a lovely mate in my life, but is always an inspiration. She is real, authentic and deeply honest in all matters and is happy to talk about them openly. She is, of course, the most talented writer and has made thousands laugh with her wit and depth and inspired many with her grounded perspective on being a woman. To me, she always seems very happy in her skin, and honest about the bits she's not so happy about; AKA the perfect person to interview for this book – and on this particular subject matter of self-love.

F: How do you feel about self-love? Although you live in America, where this turn of phrase is ubiquitous, do you think us Brits still find it slightly toe curling?

D: If I'm honest I don't really think about it in any deliberate way. I find the term a bit gooey. I suppose all it means though, is how I take care of myself. How I make sure I am happy, that I am dealing with things. So, in terms of that, I feel good about it. I'm quite real when it comes to how life works. I don't expect to be really happy all the time, or really sad. I remain as pragmatic as I can in both circumstances, and remind myself that something good, and something bad is always around the corner. You have to focus on the moment and take it for what it is.

F: Has your self-love heightened over time? I have personally found that ageing has helped me massively in this area, in a very cliché way.

D: Massively. I am about to turn 40 and I have never felt more content. I'm more at ease with everything. It's due to a few things . . . I have kids, so I don't have to wonder about whether that will happen anymore. If I want it, if I don't. I found that all quite stressful, no matter how much I tried to be relaxed about it. I found the prospect of motherhood quite daunting, like I had to get everything done before I did it, because it would ruin everything. Turns out that isn't true. I never presumed I would marry anyone, or have kids, and I was very comfortable with that, but I always worried about it, and how I would accommodate it if it did happen. I was so career driven, it was hard to imagine how it could all work together.

My other intense relationship has always been with work, but I've reached a point there where I know who I am and what I do, and am quite relaxed about it now. I don't have this constant panic that I'll never be satisfied with my work. I've realised I don't need to be famous, or make millions – as long as I get to do what I love (write) and keep my children fed, and live in a house, and have a computer to work on, then I have what I need. Don't get me wrong, I want much more than that, I love 'things' but I don't need them or feel like my happiness depends on them. As you get older, it's the essential things that matter. The clichés of health, home, happiness. Even better, if enjoyed in an amazing dress, but not the end of the world if it isn't.

Then there is my body image. I don't know how this has happened, but after two babies and approaching 40, I am happier with my body than I ever was. I think a huge part of that is that I'm not so concerned about what other people think of it, as opposed to me actually looking better. But I've realised that I don't lose any work if I put on a few pounds, my husband seems to fancy me even on a fat day and my clothes fit. I try to stay between 10 and 10 stone 5lbs because when I go much above that my clothes get tight. To maintain that weight, I get to live the life I like. I eat good food, keep active, but don't have to do anything too extreme or stick to routines that restrict me. I care about my appearance a lot, but I've never felt like my value is in what I look like. My success, and being funny, for example, have always been way more important to me.

F: What moments in life have brought up a lot of self-doubt? Have there been particular moments or circumstances where you haven't loved yourself so much?

D: Absolutely. I had a really rubbish time about 10 years ago when I was living in America to do a TV show and the show didn't happen. I ended up so broke on the other side of the world, all momentum for my career plummeted and I hardly worked for about five years. I took it really badly and got really down. I hadn't achieved what I considered to be my peak yet, and I thought I never would. I was quite defeatist about the whole thing. I look back now and want to slap my own cheeks. I had also stopped trying and just sat in a heap waiting for someone to offer me something to pull me out of it. Eventually someone did . . . a book deal. That got me back on track and with some hard work from me, things got back on a good level again. But I really disappointed myself during that time. I was on a real downer and wallowed for far too long. I basically took rejection really badly and wasn't able to see the other good things around me. Like my now husband, who I had just met. I moaned a lot in the first few years of our relationship and I regret that. I like to think I am more positive than that, but I guess everyone has their down time, and that was mine.

F: Do you have triggers that make you self-loathe or have self-doubt?

D: I write. If I don't work, I don't get paid. So when ideas dry up, or I struggle with motivation, I can worry that it will all fall apart again. But also, the fact that I categorically refuse to feel like I did during that bad time always pulls me out of it. The more I read about mental health, the more I realise that depression is a disease. I feel so much for the people I know who suffer from it, and due to their bravery and how much they talk about it to me, I know that isn't what I have. I just wallow, it's very different. And honestly, when I get down I just think what some of those people are going through and how they can't control it and I snap myself out of it. I feel like I made a choice to be miserable for a few years and I don't need to do that again.

F: What does your own negative mental Chatter sound like?

D: I mean, for me right now it's anxiety for the safety of my family. It's a new thing for me, since I had kids. I'm very happy in my life, things are going spookily well. I have to tell myself to trust it, and that it isn't all about to change. But mostly, I panic something will happen to my kids. I worry about them getting hurt, my husband dying, someone getting ill. It's so annoying. I can be feeling really happy then BAM! I imagine something awful. I take CBD gummies, do breath work and if it gets bad at night I put on a meditation on an app on my phone and eventually I fall asleep. So that's fun.

F: Do you think that anxiety is socially driven? Are we taught to fear what is going on around us? Or does your anxiety come from another place?

D: I actually probably have a much more Freudian reason for my anxiety. I lost my mum at age seven, so now somewhere inside of me, that little girl just can't believe everything will be okay. Subconsciously, I'll always think that someone's death is just around the corner. For most of my life this has been a really positive driving force behind my ambition. But now I have kids, and there is so much at stake, it comes with more fear than motivation. Of course, the state of the world doesn't help. Every time there is a school shooting, a terrorist attack, an acid attack or something else awful that the media can't sugar-coat, it only adds to the pile of things I know could go wrong.

I think anxiety is part of being a parent and that we all have various levels of it. I wish I could go back in time and apologise to every adult who was just trying to keep me safe when I was a kid, because most of the time I just thought they were being annoying.

F: How do you keep positive in everyday life?

D: I fill my life with things and keep busy. I only pick work projects I love, and I make sure I work that balance between parenting and working. I feel bad when I work too much and don't see my kids so when that feeling creeps in, I do what I can to rebalance it. I cook. Cooking makes me so happy. It's a part of my day I look forward to. I get the kids to bed, then pop in earphones and listen to an audio book as I cook dinner for me and my husband. It's my time. Cooking is a huge stress reliever for me. I also read. Reading takes you out of your head. I read fiction, and I don't really read self-help books because I want to get away from my thoughts rather than further into them. And I spend time with my husband and my friends, because they are awesome and make me so happy.

F: Finally, what do you love about yourself?

D: I have no problem with saying the things I love about myself. It's such a shame that when people admit them it's seen as arrogant, when we are being told constantly to be kinder to ourselves. So here is my list . . . I love myself as a mother. I love the way I talk to my kids, and how I show so much affection, but also discipline. I have no idea if it's the right or the wrong way, but I am happy with how I'm doing that. I love how driven I am, because it's led to a life full of really exciting opportunities and travel. I love that I cook, and host lots of parties because that brings people together and creates memories. I love my appetite, because with great food, comes great adventure. I love that I smoke pot, get drunk, read loads, listen to talk radio all day, work crazy hard, never stop making plans, say yes to opportunities, care about the world, get angry about politics, laugh at things that other people get offended by.

Now shall we do the list of things I don't love about myself? Oh, no, you didn't ask that . . . good!

F: Dawnio . . . I love ya!

Kindness Starts at Home

I do believe that self-kindness and acceptance is where we all need to start – self-love being the ultimate utopia we all hope to reach, and there's more on this a little later. Self-kindness seems a little more doable perhaps than full on LOVE as we simply start to give ourselves a break. BUT let's not forget we all came into this world full of love. Babies are pure self-love (well and crying and irregular sleep patterns and poo) as there is no self-judgement or discrimination. We all start as love. Why on earth do we deem it self-indulgent or a luxury to hold on to that state in adult life? We can and will berate ourselves for slip-ups but then we must move on and learn from that with a big slice of kindness offered up from within. The Chatter cannot survive in these moments if we truly believe in the kindness we are offering up. If we believe we don't deserve the self-punishment and self-flagellation, then the voices will quieten down. It's also not self-indulgent as, of course, everyone benefits. We can work more cohesively as a team, enter into family situations with time, love and empathy and help others in need of some love. Self-love turns into more love for others as it spreads out into the world.

Let's start to do this in the smaller moments as practice. Don't wait for a huge faux pas to try it out. If you think you could have done better at work today or could have been nicer in an overtired state while talking to your partner, forgive yourself and know you can try again tomorrow. Don't talk shit to yourself and linger on that regret, just notice it and move on. Then when any big moments hit we will all be a little more ready to apply this approach after those moments too.

I wish I had known this a while back as I could have saved endless months of inner shame and regret. I could have back all those weeks where I assumed everyone hated me and could have enjoyed so much more of my life. I had a heavy time, which I talk about a lot in my first book, *Happy*, and I know now that I could have helped along my process and pain by simply being a little less hard on myself. Much further down the line we can see that mistakes are ubiquitous, in small ways and large. We cannot avoid them or create an immunity to them, we just have to learn not to hold on to any negativity they throw up, and self-love is a big part of this.

As I have been writing this chapter, I've been thinking about how my own Inner Critic and Evil Voice work, and I have been challenging them as they pop up. This week I started work on a new TV project that I am so enjoying. It's been amazing to get back in the saddle and take back some of the control I had allowed myself to lose in this part of my career. My confidence was on the ascent and I was feeling very ready.

This did not mean I was completely head-Chatter free though: there was newness and the unknown for it to grab hold of. The Naysayer and Inner Critic were on the start line and raring to go from the moment I set foot on set.

'This lot think I'm a twat,' said my Naysayer abruptly. (This is genuinely what is going on in my head, I mean . . . what the fuck!)

'Oh, I bet they all wish it was someone else hosting, maybe Emma Willis? Yes, she would be good. I mean, I haven't done much TV over the last few years because I haven't been feeling very confident. Maybe this is all a little much for me and I should go back to the other stuff that feels less, well, out there. Damage control and all that.'

'SHUT THE FUCK UP!' was my internal reply.

I had taken note of this inner abuse and made the decision that I would implement some self-love instead. I tried to find that bit of quiet that allowed me to do so by simply breathing, focusing on just my breath and a single line of inner dialogue that simply said 'I CAN'. As cheesy and self-help book-ish as that might sound, it worked. I needed something simple and a one-liner that reminded me to be kind to myself. I then went on to thoroughly enjoy a job that I know deep down I am more than capable of.

The following day the Inner Critic piped up again to tell me I could have been perhaps a little funnier? Was I too serious or safe in my delivery due to not wanting to experiment too much on day one? Would another presenter have handled it differently? Oh god . . . here we go again!

Luckily, I managed to quieten these voices after a few minutes tolerating this familiar pattern by just giving myself a break. I could see that I had slipped in to a negative trail of thought and knew it was a waste of time. My options were: a) carry on listening to this inner drivel and end up not being my best for the rest of the series; or b) ignore the Chatter altogether and remember that I just need to be a little nicer to myself and acknowledge that I'm actually good at my job. The choice is, of course, an obvious one!

I tapped into that gut feeling that reverberated with the knowledge that I knew I was doing my best. I could have done things differently, but I didn't and that was okay because I felt the vibe was good on the day and I did what felt right in that moment. Being kinder to myself in that moment saved me perhaps a whole wasted day of mental torment which would have resulted in not much more than perhaps tense shoulders and a sleepless night to follow. Next time I'm in a bigger moment, one that feels trickier, heavier and covered in scattered words from the plethora of voices that try to run the show, I'll hopefully be able to help myself out then too. It's all about practising each time the need arises until we can quieten the voices completely, and that starts with remembering we have the choice to be kinder to ourselves.

Say Goodbye to Guilt

Another area in which self-love can really help out is guilt. Such a waste of an emotion. It never has a good outcome or drives us to do the right thing. It just sits there, name-calling at us. I sometimes feel like it's driven purely by negativity: the Inner Critic, The Voice of Others and sometimes the Evil One all love a bit of guilt to latch on to. Before I had my husband and children, this voice would tell me that I was not a good friend, daughter, sister or co-worker and then tell me all the things I could be doing better.

'Oh I should feel rather guilty about not having seen my cousin on their birthday because I chose to work instead. I really should rearrange next time to be a better person.' Such a condescending and high-horsey kind of twang to it all.

These days the voices sing in my ear whenever I'm not with my kids. Because I am freelance in all that I do there is no particular structure to my work, so often I feel like I have made a choice between work and my children in a selfish way. I was almost paralysed by it this very morning. My husband had taken the kids out for a morning of fun, while I write this book. The deadline is looming, the ideas are spinning in my head and I'm actually very excited about getting them all out and onto my laptop, but the Chatter shouts, 'Now's the time to feel very GUILTY! I have chosen to do this over being with my kids!' It brings up a physical discomfort that makes me squirm, yet I have learned to try and sit with this feeling rather than squash it with snacks and excessive cups of coffee. I just face up to the voices. I don't try and combat them with fighting talk; I just sit and wait in the quiet, and usually they go. I focus on the fact that I am really enjoying writing this book and, in turn, hopefully you'll enjoy reading it too. I concentrate on the fact that my kids see me working hard for something I really believe in and, hopefully, in turn they'll want to find their own passion in life and try new things too. I choose to look at the positives and usually the voices dull and I know my kids are happy having fun with their dad and are loved regardless of where I am.

Sitting with tricky emotions like guilt never feels good but we are also somewhat conditioned in the modern world to get the quick fix. We are told to smother any bad feelings or concerns with perhaps a quick online purchase, a convenient snack, a whizz through Instagram; any technique of distraction. If we just sit with this feeling of discomfort without running from it, we are forced to deal with it properly so next time it tries to come up it perhaps won't be so potent.

In this space between the Chatter spouting out abuse and my ability to move on from it all is a strange kind of silence. A quiet that feels too alive to be infiltrated by the mental Chatter. It's a moment where I am

fully 'feeling' what is going on rather than concentrating on my ever-chatting thoughts. My mind shuts down for this gap in time so I can assimilate what is really afoot. Is my guilt a result of being conditioned to feel it or am I confusing guilt with sadness or worry? In that quiet I attempt to just sit with those feelings and then once again give myself a little bit of kindness; to focus on the good bits and remember that once again I am trying my best. I can tap into the love that is present in the situation. The love that my husband is offering to my kids and the love that I'm pouring into this book. It's all love and has good intent so the guilt and mental Chatter can quite frankly DO ONE.

Accept Yourself

As we climb the rungs on the ladder to self-love perhaps the next level up from self-kindness is self-acceptance.

This is a time to truly acknowledge who we are and what we stand for and be at peace with it all. I was moaning to a very wise friend a while back about the small, insignificant parts of my physical body that make me feel insecure. I always self-loathe in these moments as I know I'm beyond lucky to have a fully functioning body at all but hey I'm a woman and we are unfortunately conditioned to this line of conversation. This

Here is the self-love ladder. Where are you on it right now? How could you climb the rungs to be that bit kinder to yourself? Write examples of how you could be nicer to yourself on each rung of the ladder.

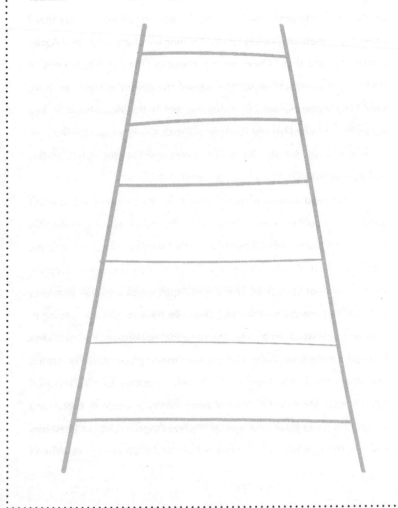

friend is extremely wise and educated on all things self-love so I was intrigued to hear her advice on how to stop the negativity more than I needed to simply vent. I was specifically moaning about the fact that I have very muscly thighs, yet I lust after long lean feminine legs. (Again, I must reiterate that I know this is pathetic and not an actual worry in life, I'm just being honest for the sake of the point I'm trying to make here.) Her response was, 'BUT Fearne, that is YOUR magic.' I looked quizzically at her to try and read into what she had just said.

She continued, 'Each part of you, exactly how it is, is YOUR magic. It's what makes you, YOU.'

I understood exactly what she meant in this moment yet couldn't grasp how I would use the information to like myself a little more in that area. Acceptance: rather than constantly listening to the Inner Critic within we must all stop lusting after what is NOT and start accepting what IS. I'm not sure there is any quick spell we can cast on ourselves to begin this mental switch-up, I think we have to just start doing it. Applying the word 'magic' to the situation worked for me as I then focused on my uniqueness and my own melting pot of idiosyncrasies and attributes that make me ME. I'm not physically Giselle, nor am I academically Stephen Fry. I'm not emotionally as adept as Oprah and I'll perhaps never be as courageous as Maya Angelou and yet I have my own strengths, quirks and, indeed, 'magic' and that feels good. When I concentrate on this, the voices die down. They start to fade like a radio going out of range until I can only hear a distant crackle and feel the warmth of my inner self-acceptance.

I'm not going to sit here and slag off social media as I love to browse and learn about other people's lives, but what we are still not very adept at is understanding how unnatural it is for us to know so much about others. Rewind only 10 years and we had no such looking glass to hold up to others. We had no idea what everyone else was doing/wearing/eating. It is hard to accept ourselves in the modern world as we are so used to seeing so many other options or ways to be. The 'like' button doesn't help in these situations as we think we are also seeing what is popular. We may even confuse this with what is 'right'. This is the part that scares me for the younger generations out there who have grown up with only this model to learn from.

Popularity doesn't mean better or right or perfect or correct. Photos and social media posts can of course get 'likes' because they're shocking or unbelievable and not necessarily because they are adored by the masses. Even if they were, those moments or posts are no more important than you and your life. They aren't bigger or better: they're just seen more. The strange smoke and mirrors that surrounds social media does make self-acceptance tougher but not impossible. We must all always route back to what FEELS right to us. If our line of work, body shape, style, tastes, opinions and passions differ to those that are deemed 'important' on social media, it doesn't devalue them. If no one else is dressing in the same way, sharing information in the same way or discussing subjects in the same way it doesn't make them null and void. We must understand the worth of our own magic and sometimes that is a rarity. Maybe that makes it even more special. Our magic!

Not valuing oneself is a bad habit all of us can get into. We compare and despair and the mental Chatter tells us our values don't count. It's a dirty trap to fall into but very easy in this day and age. We must all grab hold of our own unique magic, no matter how varied it appears to others, and own it. That's when others start to see the value in it too. It shines out of us and compels others to break moulds and routine and relax into their own magic too. It can even start movements. Look at those who inspire you – I'm pretty sure they'll be the ones leading the crowds rather than following them. See worth in your own ideas and remember your own magic.

Can I again just clarify that 'magic' isn't amazing leggy legs, or the IQ of the brainiest brain box, it's your own thing, whatever that might be and however that might feel and look. It's my weird little ears that look like Findus Crispy Pancakes (they really do!); it's my veiny translucent skin; my extreme knowledge of all things Led Zeppelin; it's my need for detail and my passion to learn. It's all of me.

What is your magic? It doesn't have to be the 'good' bits, it's the weird, the wonderful, the unique, the YOU! Write your list here.

First Comes Love

So onto the 'love' bit. The holy grail on this treacherous and at times uncomfortable expedition. I used to hate it when people (my husband) would offer up the well-used line of advice, 'you can't love another unless you love yourself'. It used to rile me to the point of eye rolling and buttock clenching. I didn't want to hear it as I really didn't love myself at all. Maybe I don't fully yet, but I'm certainly more aware of why I struggle in areas and I'm also much more comfortable liking the other bits. I might hear those voices rear up to highlight the negative but knowing that it's just Chatter and not the full truth allows me to not take it all so seriously.

That chunk of advice is hard to swallow as it's so black and white, but I guess if we really look at the meaning behind it, we can see the true information offered up. Love is not just about giving; it is also the receiving. It is a full-circle experience that needs to feel fluid and ever-moving to work. We can give all of our love to others but if we don't love/accept/act kindly to ourselves we won't get the return, so then our own offered up love turns to resentment or sorrow or perhaps more self-loathing. We can attempt to take love from others but if we are not giving it out and feeling it from within then we will end up

pushing it further away. It has to keep moving in a circular motion and that must start from within us. This is of course another opportunity for our mind Chatter to pipe up, especially if we have been hurt before.

The Voice of Others can linger and ricochet around our skulls for years, and often lifetimes. Sometimes it is very hard indeed to change a narrative that you have lived by over a stretch of years. If we have been told we are unlovable, unloved or incapable of loving, it can be tricky to rid yourself of this notion. The Voice of Others will surreptitiously plant previously spoken words in our heads as if we are purely defined by them, breathing life into old and stagnant wounds to make us believe they have bearing on us now. This voice can hold us back a lot where love is concerned and is usually extremely prevalent for most of us where self-love is concerned too.

Can you think of a moment from your past where someone has told you you weren't good enough? I have had relationships ended by others many a time. Sometimes partners in life and at other times friendships. It is hard not to take these moments personally and feel not-enough. In my twenties, a short-lived romance was ended via text. There I was at a friend's house, watching TV, when my phone pinged to alert me to the fact that I was not lovable any more. It took me a while to get out of a very negative mindset after this as I wasn't expecting it and also wasn't ready for this knockback. My internal Chatter oscillated between the Angry Voice who was ready with a lengthy, punchy and at times hilariously seething rants, to the Inner Critic telling me that I, indeed, was very unlovable and should perhaps change to rectify this. The Angry One's words and phrases would never be spoken aloud, but felt good to riff around mentally – for a while anyway. The Inner Critic kept me feeling low. Any self-love or optimism for the future was certainly diminished.

At this point in my life, the natural remedy to it all was luckily great friends, the odd night out dancing and then gradually remembering how good it felt to flirt with others. The negativity that danced around that short, sharp text message started to veer off and leave me alone as I started to remember all the things I loved about me rather than what somebody else claimed to. I found that self-love in the quiet that appeared from the distraction of great friends. If we are feeling a little low on the self-love meter, good friends can help remind us how bloody brilliant we truly are. They can coax out our fun side, our naughty side and help celebrate the parts of us that another tried to shun. Let others help you on your road to self-love.

The power of self-love. It can be incredibly healing all round.

We must also remember that self-love isn't driven by ego, it's about feeling. We can, of course, use little positive mantras or phrases to help us along the way; words that boost us and make us believe we are able to

Write a list here of all the small things you like about yourself.
A minimum of five! GO!

love and be loved, but real self-love doesn't need a full-on inner dialogue and isn't driven by us acting entitled due to how bloody brilliant we think we are. It's a softer love than that and a lot more peaceful.

It's a state of mind that allows us to act courageously (more on this in Chapter 4) but also without hurting others or closing off from what's really going on. We may still get hurt or be told difficult things in life but if we like ourselves from within it'll be that bit easier to get over them and move on to accept love again.

Can we start perhaps by loving a bit of ourselves, if not fully then perhaps incrementally, building up strength and momentum as we go? Do you love your ability to make friends easily? To adapt and move with change? Do you love your aptitude for helping others or perhaps the way you can turn measly leftovers into a great meal? There'll be something we can all start with. I'll perhaps start you off with my own moment of self-reflection and scrambling for the good bits. I love the way I am able to get lots done. I have a lot of drive and passion and that, in turn, fuels my energy and makes me incredibly enthusiastic about certain areas of my life. These are moments where I feel fully alive. I used to wish I was a more chilled out person who could drift through situations without this fire and need but I have grown to really love these qualities I have and see them as my magic.

I love that I'm a nurturer. I adore looking after people, cooking up warm meals for them and sending small gifts. I'm thankful I'm naturally like this and feel happy and not arrogant in admitting it. I also love that although I've been hurt, pushed aside and at times floored by cirumstance, I have always tried again. I may be bruised by exerience but I'm bouncy and resilient too. I love that I'm like this.

I guess self-love is a strange and complex alchemy of forgiving ourselves for our past mistakes, honouring our true nature, remembering we are our own worst critic and diminishing the brutal chat we throw at ourselves when the negative Chatter sparks up. Maybe we can't always tick all of the above boxes but if we are at least working on a couple of them at a time we stand a good chance in getting to that place of full, glorious self-love.

I strive to accept and love myself without my Chatter telling me I need this from others.

4

Quiet Courage

When we think of the word 'courage', it usually conjures up an image of firefighters putting their own life on the line to save others or perhaps the suffragettes facing public discrimination to make huge social change. It's about people that have put another person or a cause before their own life. Of course, it can be all of these important and intense things – but it can also be so much smaller and within us all. We have all met or encountered heroes or heroism in our lifetimes. Witnessing friends switch up their lives to change career later in life or seeing our own children stepping nervously into a new school in shiny black shoes. Courage comes in many shapes and sizes.

Spotting Our Own Courage

It might feel almost cringeworthy to acknowledge our own courageous moments and sometimes impossible to believe there have been any at all, but look hard enough and they're there. For a Brit, admitting that we have previously been courageous feels as uncomfortable as saying we love/like ourselves. We dull down past achievements or milestones while apologising profusely along the way. Why is it that we say 'sorry', when really we mean 'please can you get out of my way'? We are a strange breed. Anyway, I digress.

Maybe you are a local hero or have a job which involves regular heroism? Maybe you save lives in your line of work or have to take great risks? For the most of us who aren't and don't, courage can feel sparse and sporadic with more room available for routine and our comfort zones. Sometimes, though, courage has been present even if we weren't quite aware of it at the time. It doesn't have to be all 'leaping in front of moving traffic to rescue another' but can be found woven throughout our lives in much quieter and gentler moments. Have you asked someone on a date? Perhaps called someone up to say sorry? Or tried a new hobby? All these moments involve personal courage and a willingness to step out of our comfort zones.

The common link between all courageous moments, no matter how big or small, is 'risk'. As much as we like to believe that we are in control in our day-to-day lives with our ticking clocks, synced iCals and mapped-out schedules, we really are dicing with risk most of the time. We are more aware of this if we are willing to live in the moment without trying to micromanage every second – then we can see the risk that lies in our everyday lives. But rather than being scared of that risk, let's try to see what opportunity can come from it. Living courageously and ready for newness. Ready to act dynamically and responsibly without too much fear and worry. Sometimes I actually quite like feeling a bit nervous or unsure of what is about to go down as I feel ever so alive. If I'm about to interview someone I have never met for my podcast series there is risk afoot. My courage comes in the form of going with the flow and accepting the unknown. It could be a cracking interview with fluidity and revelation, or it could be stagnant and full of silent gaps. I have to jump into that space and just see what happens. Fun fear perhaps?

Some days, I wake up naturally feeling ready for the unknown, ready for whatever comes my way. Excited. Yet of course there are days where I am the opposite of this. A slug in a tracksuit coasting through a grey Tuesday shut off from human connection and glued to my phone to disconnect from the pain and joy of reality. The mental Chatter, the Lazy One, holds me in this space, debilitated and unable to activate my inner courage. My heart is dull and it seems I am responsive only to that negativity.

Connecting with others, stepping out of our comfort zone, seeking newness, all takes courage as it's stepping into the unknown. It takes courage to be a human as we have no idea what is going to happen and when. Most of us are scared and most of us feel anxiety at some point, so getting up and showing up require courage – and a nice slice of quiet in the brain department can really help here. We can so easily talk ourselves out of newness and adventure but if we recognise again that it's just the habitual negative Chatter going off on one, we can try to counteract it. We can use thought and phrases to get us up and get us ready for action. We can stop and remember that we all feel a little scared and none of us know what is really going on, and we can switch up the inner chat. Rather than focusing on the negative outcomes I think of the positive 'what ifs'. What if this turns out to be amazing!? What if I meet someone incredible today? What if today brings adventure? 99 per cent of the time the things we are terrified of never end up happening and even if they do, even if we end up looking a fool, making a mistake, or not doing our best, at least we know that we showed up and tried! That, I think, is more important than anything.

HELLO TO . . . SARAH OUTEN

A few years ago my great friend, Kris Hallenga, posted me a book called *A Dip in the Ocean* (knowing that I could receive no greater gift than a book – Fearne Bookworm Cotton/Wood) about her friend, Sarah Outen. I took this book off on holiday with me as at this point I had no children so could actually read a whole book on holiday. I raced through its pages and imbibed every tantalising and sometimes terrifying story about Sarah's solo crossing of the Indian Ocean in her small one-person boat. She did this at only 23 years of age so my mind boggled as to how she conjured up such courage to take on such a feat completely on her own. No one to fall back on in lonely moments; no one to grab hold of in mountainous waves. Unimaginable. Of course, this was not enough for Sarah so she began plotting her next adventure which was again a solo trip but this time around the whole world on bike, kayak and sail boat. Venturing off into the unknown – new countries, language barriers and no guarantees – with excitement rather than dread. To say I was inspired reading this book is the biggest understatement. It's highly unlikely I'll ever cycle from Calais to the most easterly point in Russia or get in a kayak anytime soon, but there are lessons to be learned for us when reading about Sarah's courage and positive attitude – she's the perfect person to quiz for this book.

F: Sarah, your book, *A Dip in the Ocean*, had a lasting effect on me. I so admire your strength and sheer courage in achieving such a feat and in such circumstances. At the start of your first solo voyage, how were you feeling and what Chatter did you hear from within?

S: Thanks Fearne. It had taken me three hard years to get to the start of my Indian Ocean row – powered by a belief and conviction from who knows where and all the naivety of a 23 year old. It also marked three years since my Dad died very suddenly, so it represented a journey through the first years of grief and loss, too. By the time I made it to Australia, I felt focused, proud to have got there, utterly exhausted and nervous about all the unknowns ahead. That said, the first time I saw the ocean in all its massiveness, I felt very small and not so certain of myself. So I played to my strengths of keying in to the rational and logical part of me and not spending too much energy on anything else. I had always been very driven and determined, good at dampening or ignoring my emotions and I was, I suppose, afraid of failure. In the final 24 hours before departure, I felt the nerves rising and tried even more to focus in on the essentials, talking to myself in my head and out loud, too. When nervous feelings arose, I tried talking to them as I would a nervous child, reassuring myself that I was doing my best, that I was well-prepared and that my boat was going to look after me. In fact, that we were going to look after each other.

On setting out it felt good to be moving, to be on my way and looking back at the huge effort – emotional, physical, logistical and so on – that it had taken to get there. But I was also seasick and exhausted, hallucinating for the first couple of days such that I had to tell the 'people' in my boat to get off. As it happens, a change in weather and an electrical issue forced me back to shore after 10 days and I remember that first attempt being full of negative Chatter and worry about what other people might be thinking from afar, watching my GPS track returning home. I named it my 'Warm-Up Lap' and went back out to sea a week later! My attitude to the voices in and out of my head was to hear them but not to listen to them if they didn't serve me (easier said than done sometimes).

F: The journey was a complete roller coaster, of course, and had huge ups and downs. How did your Chatter react in these moments?

S: Ups and downs and upside downs! One of the most important lessons I have learned from the ocean (and am still glad to be reminded of) is that nothing lasts forever – every storm will eventually pass. Sometimes that is helpful to remember and repeat to myself in rough weather, though often that comes with retrospect and getting through something turbulent.

My Chatter is often really quiet in the good times and high points – it only seems to get chatty when I am nervous or struggling. I consciously talk to myself when things are challenging or I need to keep focus or stay awake.

Around three months in I capsized for the first time, and was really shaken. I had been outside emptying out the bilge when we were hit by a big wave and over we went into the washing machine. When the boat righted I couldn't get back on board because my safety line (which had just saved my life) had got caught around the gate where the oar sits. So to get back on board, I had to undo the line and scramble back on, holding on for my life. If I had been capsized during that time of being unclipped, I wouldn't be writing this to you today. I was very calm – something instinctive kicked in and kept me safe. It was later on as the shock dissipated that I got emotional and battled with wanting to stay inside the cabin. I had to focus on being pragmatic while also trying to parent the tiny me that was terrified, I suppose. That's the thing I recognise in my solo voyages – and to an extent on land in 'normal life', too – that I have to be all the different characters in a team.

F: Being on your own is scary to many but to be completely on your own for so long seems unimaginable to most. Did that solitude heighten your inner dialogue and how did you remain feeling grounded and sane?

S: My inner dialogue is often outer too! I talk to myself a lot and also to my boat, the animals that pass by. It's very social out there – in my head at least – and for me that chance to be in solitude is really beautiful. There's plenty of tough stuff too and I find that there can be no escape from negative Chatter at times. When I struggled with it, I would try and do something different for a bit – like wash my hair or read a letter from home or cook something nice to eat. I know that I can be my worst critic at times, saying things to myself that I wouldn't say to anyone else, so I know that to get the best out of myself I need to be my biggest champion too, when I can.

I think that being out at sea in a tiny rowing boat is very grounding – it is all about trying to be present and 'in the moment'. Often that awareness comes very organically and easily and my mind is a bit like what I imagine Winnie the Pooh's to be like – thoughts wandering in and out, as and when they please, but not being too bothered by them. At other times, it can be more difficult to stay present. I have only started meditating in a formal way in the last few years but I think I was meditating years before I knew what it was, coming into the body to check in with the different parts of it and how they are feeling. It felt a bit like a team manager checking in with all the crew. 'Hello Toes, how are you doing? Legs, what's going on for you right now?' and so on. Contact with home was important too – human-to-human connections are so important, even and maybe especially in solitude.

During tricky times I recited poems I had learned and sung songs out loud. At the end of every day I would shout out 'Good Things About Today' and list at least one thing that was good. During stormy weather I would often try and actively zone out, imagining myself somewhere other than my stinking, wet cabin being thrown around in the ocean. I held onto a thumb stone my mum had given me – rubbing its smoothness to sooth myself.

F: In tricky and dangerous times did you have an inner cheerleader who gave you strength and got you through the worst?

S: Yes! Partly instinctive and partly consciously playing different roles to look after me, make decisions, check I was looking after myself and so on or soothing the fear.

F: With no one else around and no one to talk to what did you learn about yourself and notice about how you think?

S: I learned that I sometimes find it harder to motivate myself alone than when I am with others and can talk myself out of things very well at times . . . I also learned that, for all my love of solitude and finding it generally comes very easy to me, I do really value time with others, too.

F: Did the quiet open you up to much more awareness of what was going on around you?

S: Yes, and in the good times that was beautiful, sublime and almost magical. There was something very exhilarating about being solo in more challenging conditions and I felt that closeness to my own feelings of fear and frustration perhaps even more strongly than had I been with another person.

F: With only survival and travelling in a direction on your mind, did you find the more flippant worries and concerns faded into the background?

S: I love that about expedition life, how everything simplifies into staying alive, well and making progress or reducing collateral. There's obviously a bit more to it than that (weather/equipment/route, etc.) but I find it a much easier space and state of mind to be present and aware than at home.

F: How do you deal with mental Chatter in everyday life? Have you found your own personal way to mitigate its potency?

S: I'm still working on this one . . . I have had various depressive episodes and PTSD responses to traumatic stuff in the last few years and at the lowest ebbs my head is a raging, frightening torrent of self-battering venom. I try and think about what my fictional character A.N. Other would do or say to those voices. I find yoga, meditation, mantras and exercise all really helpful too.

F: When you were on your London-to-London around-the-world trip, you tapped into your intuition regularly. You managed to know when to trust some strangers along the way who offered comfort or a roof over your head for the night and when to turn and bolt. How do you consistently do this and not let mental Chatter get in the way?

S: There's a lot to be said for instinct and rationale, though that said sometimes bad things can happen to people, whether we are at home or not. Trusting your instinct and trusting that it will keep you safe is sometimes difficult and perhaps comes with practice, too. I think that rationalising fear – in this instance, of others – can be an important tool. That said, I often think 'What would I do if X, Y or Z happened right now' and if ever I felt unsafe I would make moves to get away from a situation.

F: Some out there reading this will find it very hard to meet new people. It becomes quite an overwhelming fear. When you're on the road for so long and you're meeting new people constantly how do you initiate those moments where you knock on a stranger's door to ask for water or start chatting to someone new? Where does that courage come from?

S: I, too, find it hard to meet new people in certain situations and in certain times in my life, so I relate to that shyness, fear or whatever the name is. To an extent a degree of caution and wariness is probably a good, useful thing as it lets you tune into your intuition and instinct. Smiling is a universal expression and letting people see your eyes, removing a bike helmet etc. is helpful – and not being afraid to make polite excuses (or more!) and retreat if something doesn't feel right. Most of all remember that 99.99999999 per cent of people are good people and want to do well by you. And give yourself a pep talk/practise what you would like to say and try and be present in your body so that you can actively relax tense muscles – all these things can help me when I'm nervous.

F: Sarah, you unstoppable force of nature, THANK YOU!

Courage in Love

If you are finding it hard to remember your own previous courageous moments let me ask you this: have you ever fallen in love? Has time stopped as you looked at another for the first time, or has it slowly crept in to your life like a warm breeze as you gradually fell for a partner or new best friend? If the answer is 'yes', even if unrequited, then you have, indeed, been courageous.

Is there anything more unknown than stepping towards another you feel you have a connection with? You often know little about this new, intoxicating person yet the emotion that swarms around you when in their presence is inexplicable and other-worldly. You may not be able to write out a 'pros and cons' list of whether you should step even closer because the heart and gut have taken over and the head feels foggy. Any negative Chatter is minimal in these moments as the heart sends a signal to the negativity to piss right off. There is no room for those downer voices to have their say as something much bigger is afoot: LOVE. GLORIOUS! Isn't falling in love the best?

It has been written about relentlessly over the years and some even refer to it as a madness due to its intoxicating qualities. It can almost feel like our brains have been rewired in those first moments of love as we actually start to think differently and act differently too. Of course, it doesn't always work out how we had imagined; I have certainly been burned on several occasions. I have taken the risk, put everything into what I believed would be a future of union and it hasn't panned out in the way I had envisaged. That is where the jeopardy lies. We may have heart-palpitating feelings coursing through our bodies convincing us that this person and risk is the right option but there are of course no guarantees. Even in those situations where things haven't worked out I have little regret in taking the plunge. I have enjoyed the roller coaster of emotions, because once again I felt very alive, and I know that in those moments I followed my heart. And sometimes it does work out – which proves courage is worth it. If only all courageous acts batted the Chatter out of the way as easily as love does. I find it so much harder with the smaller moments of courage. The risks that I know could benefit me in the long run but perhaps feel too arduous or difficult to bother with.

SOAR

ABOVE IT ALL

Taking Risks

As I mentioned earlier, I have recently started getting myself properly back into TV, which I am massively excited about, yet find slightly scary and risky, too. It might seem over the top to use the word 'courage' here as I'm not saving lives or risking my own to make this show happen, but there were a lot of unknown factors and so I did worry if my negative Chatter would try to sabotage it for me. For quite a few years now I have felt a little too scared and perhaps delicate to dive back into TV. I worked relentlessly in that medium from the age of 15, well into my late twenties, and then hit some personal road bumps. Emotionally and mentally, I hit a wall and that lead to a heightened awareness of my own mental Chatter and a big lack of confidence. I assumed everyone was thinking I was rubbish as I kept listening to the Evil One's acerbic tones daily. I panicked when faced with newness as again those voices upstairs told me I wasn't good enough and would be mocked greatly for any further efforts.

I felt a new and exciting comfort in writing books and working on the design projects I so love, though. These parts of my working life felt comfortable and cosy and also a little bit secretive. I could squirrel away on these projects with little disturbance from others. My work would still be judged and criticised – but at a distance. Being on the TV during this time felt too raw and exposing. I did still continue working on shows I felt very at ease with but my mental Chatter would not allow me to try anything that felt like a risk. On the few occasions that I did dip my toe into new waters I felt such panic that it was perhaps a little early for me to be courageous. In some circumstances this lead to actual panic attacks which were a shock and all new to me at the age of 36. Physical panic. Heart-racing, skin-prickling panic, all wrapped up in the mental concern that I knew I was about to faint. Really fun, right!

After 21 years on the TV, I wasn't expecting this to come out of the blue. It ended up being much more to do with the other responsibilities and stresses in my life, but the 'new' bit of the jobs I was working on were the straw that finally broke the TV presenter's back. My negative Chatter told me it was just the fact that I was trying something new on the TV and that I shouldn't be doing it as I wasn't good enough, whereas really I was just pushed to the max in every corner of my life. Once again I was trying to do too much. Negativity doesn't like common sense so went for the dramatic option of trying to debilitate me while at work instead.

Recently I have been facing up to the Chatter and questioning a lot of what it is presenting me with. Somehow I had allowed its voice and vehement words to wipe out years and years of practice and hard work.

These words were so potent that I believed them and let countless hours of live TV and broadcasting crumble to an insignificant pile of rubble, topped with a few of the cruellest tweets from others and slurs from uppity TV critics. Why had I allowed this to happen?

I could sit there and blame the handful of people that have taken the time to send their vitriolic words my way, or I could remember the countless times when I have felt a buzz of achievement when a broadcast has gone well. I could sit and listen to the Chatter and feel weaker by the day or I could get myself back out there and give it a bloody good go again. A risk, no matter how small, still takes courage. I knew I would have to work hard to dampen the efforts of the mental Chatter when I was on set as I didn't want to waste time constantly worrying about what every cameraman and production member was thinking of me. The mental Chatter would, of course, try to whisper in my ear mid-sentence on camera that everyone thought I was shit at my job but I couldn't let this stop me from progressing in a job I actually really love. I often find that with presenting, and probably most moments that involve talking aloud, half the job is quieting the voices in our heads with the sound of the voice coming out of our mouths. It can be uncomfortable to most to speak aloud as there is instant judgement and you're putting yourself out there. Once again just showing up and having a go takes courage.

So to get to the crux of it, I said a big fat YES to this new job and

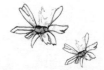

so far I'm really enjoying it. I have come to accept that of course some people will love the show, some might not so much. Some might enjoy what I have to say, some will think I'm a twat. The outcome must remain irrelevant to me as I have made the leap and taken the risk and all in goodwill. The brain Chatter was, in this case, defeated as I said YES even when risk was involved and I did feel a teeny bit courageous. I'm no firefighting hero but it was a small personal victory which I think will now act as the impetus for so much more in both my working and personal lives. Sometimes courage can breed courage.

Harness the Quiet

In that small chunk of time from the moment we are asked to be a part of something new or, indeed, have a light-bulb moment or idea, to the time it takes to say 'YES I'M IN', there lies a silence. Whether the task at hand requires monumental courage or a thin slither of the stuff, there is a moment; a chasm in time where no thoughts form and the head almost shuts down. The quiet! The gut activates and sparks up a response, if we let it, that can extinguish fear and concern in one fell swoop: courage. We may have made 400 pros and cons lists beforehand or had sleepless nights in the lead up to reaching that final pivotal moment but in those few seconds right before we say 'YES', there is nothing. A glorious pause in a stop-motion scene of our lives. We are hanging over the edge of newness, yet deep down we might just know it's okay to freefall into the unknown. It's in this moment we can truly understand that negative habits may have tried to swerve us off the path of exploration and risk-taking wonder, but really its manifesto stood no chance as the gut had the answer all along.

When we listen to those negative voices that like to challenge courage – the Naysayer and the Lazy One – we clip our own wings, sometimes to the extreme of forgetting we can fly. We lessen the room we have to move around in as the Chatter tells us we shouldn't try newness, trust the unknown or say that powerful word: 'YES'. We see less, experience less and learn less in the process. Courage always leads to one of the aforementioned and sometimes all three. Leaping into the unknown will certainly make us see so much more as we are in a slightly heightened state. We are perhaps on alert or aware of the newness around us. We of course then experience new adventures in life which leads to self-exploration and in turn learning. Even if the outcome isn't what was imagined, the learning bit will, of course, still happen. If the career change didn't go to plan, the new partner didn't work out or the attempt at a new hobby was short-lived, you still took the risk and tried. You let courage be the driving force and can still celebrate the victory of not letting the mental Chatter take over and win. Remember you've done it before. I've done it before. We can all do it again!

Don't Let Failure Keep You Down

Let's revisit failure for a moment and its richness and importance in life. It takes vast amounts of courage to fail and even more to pick ourselves back up in the aftermath and sift through the debris to notice the valuable lessons learned. No one likes talking about failure. It can be embarrassing and toe curling and hideous to recall. It can leave us feeling bathed in shame and regret and can be used by our negative voices to talk us out of future moments.

We can either listen to the Chatter after a moment of despair and humiliation and allow it to ward us off any future risk taking or exploration, or we can stick our middle finger up to it and try again. We can find the gems among the dirt and rubble and take those lessons learned on to our next adventure. We can enter into new challenges with a knapsack full of experience that we can draw on if things get tough, using past moments of failure and pain to remind us of our own strength. Remembering we have a choice and that we do not need to concentrate on the accusatory reproaches of our mental Chatter after failure allows us to once again take risks and be courageous. It's almost like a checklist of things we need to remember in these moments.

Point 1

Remember that everyone has failed at some point. Even people we admire, people who look to have it all sussed, have failed along the way.

Point 2

Failure means you took a risk and beat the Chatter in the first place.

Point 3

Failure doesn't mean you are a failure. We don't have to embody this experience and be defined by it forever. The Chatter will try to hook us into believing so, but we all know deep down that it isn't true. We will only ever be failures if we stop moving forward with our guts and hearts and only listen to our negativity telling us lies.

'But what if OTHERS have branded us a failure?' I hear you cry. Well, yes I have been on the receiving end of this in some areas of my life and again the middle finger comes in handy for this one. Why does

Write down five negative things about your life now, and then for each negative point write down three positive things to help you override it.

NEGATIVE ....

POSITIVE *1* ....

POSITIVE *2* ....

POSITIVE *3* ....

NEGATIVE ....

POSITIVE *1* ....

POSITIVE *2* ....

POSITIVE *3* ....

NEGATIVE ....

POSITIVE *1* ....

POSITIVE *2* ....

POSITIVE *3* ....

NEGATIVE ....

POSITIVE *1* ....

POSITIVE *2* ....

POSITIVE *3* ....

NEGATIVE ....

POSITIVE *1* ....

POSITIVE *2* ....

POSITIVE *3* ....

another's opinion mean more than our own? Why should someone else's words have more potency and punch than what we truly believe of ourselves? We may feel defeated and beaten down by others' words, but it will only take hold if we listen to the negativity telling us that it means more than what we truly believe.

'But, hold your horses again, what if I DO believe the same to be true? What if I don't believe I am good enough or capable of more?' I hear you emphatically ask. This is tricky, but it is yet again only down to patterns of thought and bad habits. None of us are failures, or not good enough, we have just got into negative patterns of behaviour that'll take some time to rectify, like trying to twist a reluctant Rubik's cube into the right formation. It isn't impossible, yet may take time.

My friend Zephyr Wildman, who I mentioned earlier, always reminds me that it takes five good thoughts to replace one negative. That means more effort is needed to beat this vicious cycle, but my god, isn't it worth it? I think most good things in life require a little discipline. That doesn't mean there has to be a battle to make changes but there is a requirement for attention and sometimes a lot of letting go.

Letting go of negative thought patterns can be tough as they feel comfy, like a favourite sweater we've had for years. We feel at home in its distressed and worn appearance and don't see need for change, even when we know it's for the best. This is where a bit of affirmation comes into play. We have to copy and paste new sentences in the place of old ones, even if they are a little scripted at first. So when the Naysayer Voice pops up to tell us we should never take another risk again in case we fail, we have to Tippex it out of our minds and write over in thick marker pen: 'I can try again. I can be courageous.'

Even if these new positive lines feel inauthentic at first, with practice they'll become that bit more real, in exactly the same way your mind has, up until now, only believed the rehearsed and practised negative lines.

You Can Always Escape

Have you ever said the word 'yes' out loud and wondered where it came from? I certainly have and these moments are exciting, yet shit scary, as it's almost as if someone else has said it. Sometimes the 'yes' may come out as an 'oh, go on then', as you're still in the midst of convincing yourself something is a good idea. A bungee jump on holiday or even a spin around the dance floor at a wedding with a stranger when you hate dancing. Sometimes the courage kicks in before the negative Chatter can get started up. We can tap into that gut feeling and inner knowledge without the negative getting too involved. These

Imagine you are the circle. If you are feeling trapped by certain situations write down what they are in each box. After you've written each one down imagine the boxes moving further away from the circle in the middle. Can you make any changes to these blocks or is there any way of accepting them a little more to give yourself some freedom?

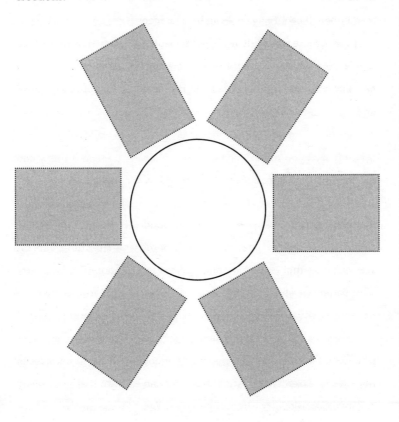

smaller moments of courage are just as important as the BIG yesses that might be life changing. They remind us that we are dynamic and ever-changing and that we can move into new areas of life whenever we need to.

Our negative Chatter encourages us all to believe we are trapped in life. Have you ever felt trapped? In a relationship, friendship, work or geographical area? Usually, the Chatter will have reinforced any personal beliefs afoot and will have convinced you that you are caged in circumstance. The Naysayer Voice will trick you into thinking that change would mean being disloyal or weak willed and would most certainly lead you to nothing but misery. Feeling trapped is shitty and can be seriously ramped up by this negativity. We might believe we will never find a partner better than the one we have now when in an unhappy relationship. The Chatter tells us that if we break free and set off in a new direction with courage by our side we'll more than likely end up alone forever. That critical gut feeling gets smothered in the Naysayer's clammy words and dulls it down to the point of non-existence. It's so easy to end up in a situation like this. Courage takes practice and when we are out of touch with it of course it'll always be easier to listen to negativity and just stay put. Courage is almost like a muscle we need to keep flexing so it remains nimble and dynamic and ready to use whenever great change is needed. The gut may not come with

Colour in the top half of this head in any colour that first pops into your mind. Now sit comfortably and close your eyes and visualise this colour in the space in between your eyes. Let thoughts come and go without judgement by concentrating on this colour.

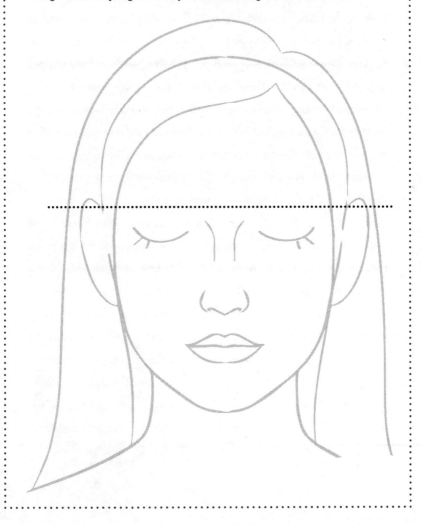

a vast vocabulary but sometimes it might just throw out a 'what if' to the mental Chatter to challenge its pompous mandate. If we get more practised at listening to that tiny 'what if' and start to see it as an exciting challenge rather than an opportunity to look for problems then we can start to follow our guts more and not get shut down by the negative. 'What if' I do meet another brilliant person in my lifetime? 'What if' I do manage to start a new career years down the line? 'WHAT IF' gives us the chance to step outside of our usual negative thought patterns and allows us to play a little positive and fun game. Tiny steps towards courage! Gradually that 'what if' might just become an emphatic 'YES' as we get better at sailing into uncharted waters.

Courage can seem like something that is only needed in extreme circumstances, but really it can be in our lives every day. We can use it to stop the negative patterns and the Chatter we have all at times adhered to.

I know I have
been courageous
before so I know
I can be again.

5

Quiet Trust

Throughout history people have been placing their fate and destiny into the hands of gods or icons that they believe will help, support and manifest the good stuff. Many of you might still place most of your trust and faith into a particular methodology or religious structure and that I'm sure feels particularly healing. But what about the rest of us who haven't pinned all belief in one particular faith? How do we trust that everything will be okay? And what do we trust in? Where do we find our well of inner strength from? And can we learn to trust when society often tells us we shouldn't? Often we are presented with quite a scary version of what is happening on planet Earth and that makes it hard to know who to trust. Trusting in something or someone or even ourselves can, of course, instantly bring in some quiet and allow us to stop the ever-chattering mental worry and fear we feel.

Finding the Source

I find it difficult to define what I believe in as I'm not always completely sure myself. As I stumble down this path of learning and self-discovery I enjoy hearing stories from different cultures and religions and perhaps subconsciously use different parts of those varying methodologies. It makes me slightly wince to say I am 'spiritual' but I guess that best sums it up. I do indeed believe there is some sort of magic afoot that we can tap in to if we are in the right frame of mind. I don't believe that we are just solid matter floating about in outer space without purpose or something other than just what is visible to us. Perhaps there is magic or energy we can't see, or touch or even explain. This concept might not be pinned to one particular god or idea but I do believe there is something out there or perhaps actually within us that we can tap in to when we aren't busying ourselves with worry and concern about the minutiae of modern living. The place where miracles shock us, great strength is drawn and love sprouts like weeds. If you think that I'm bordering on hippie with this and can't get on board with there being much else apart from what we see around us, then maybe you can recognise moments where you have felt utter joy from being in nature, or a deep security from the love of others, and that is a comfort and magic in itself?

I often wonder if this is the place or source of energy from which I can extract hope when needed. Sometimes I will call upon it in horrific times when all seems broken but it's also the place where I can summon up ideas that excite and buzz, and trust they'll be brought to life. Some days it feels effortless. I may be in a particularly good mood for no particular reason and have an idea while I'm out running. I'll then activate my inner hope or, indeed, draw it from this magical and unknown well (who knows where it comes from?) and feel the strength and confidence that I can make it happen. I will be aware that there is work ahead and that I will need to put certain wheels in motion but beneath that there are the foundations of hope and trust, otherwise I probably wouldn't bother at all.

On those days, or in fact weeks, where I am not feeling sprightly and naturally hopeful, I do find the whole process that bit trickier. Without having a god or figure who has a holy name to call up and chat to I feel a little lost. Who will support me in uncertain times and who will help to extinguish my negative voices telling me I'm headed down a one way street of doom? It is probably me. I'm the one that can create that change and as previously mentioned in the 'Self-Love' and 'Courage' chapters, I can trust in myself. I can believe that I will find the strength to make change when needed and if I'm really struggling I will call out to those who I know love me to help me in the process.

Trust Yourself . . .

I don't know about you but when I'm in an uncertain situation I feel very out of control. I am a classic, cliché Virgo. A clock-watching and punctual, surface-cleaning, control freak. When left awaiting answers or when feeling unsure, I get completely strung out and my negative Chatter loves these moments. There is expansive time and space that this negativity knows it can fill with tonnes of useless Chatter.

When I left Radio 1 after 10 years of security, which by no means did I take for granted, I had no plans at all. No fallback, no support elsewhere, just a big empty calendar of nothingness. With a lot of responsibility and children to care for I swayed between euphoric and adventurous optimism to complete and utter terror. My fear churned up those negative voices and it would keep me awake for hours (more on sleep later!). I would be in that heavenly descent towards the black and numb of sleep and then they would whisper in my ear that I had made a terrible mistake: I now meant nothing to the artists I had spent years working with and had lost my place forever in the music industry which I had lusted after for so many years beforehand. The combative side of me would shout loudly 'NOT NOW! I NEED SLEEP', which usually made the mental Chatter splutter out acerbic sentences of self-doubt in quicker succession. I had to trust the moment in which the initial idea to leave that security was formed. The idea had come from me, I was quite clear on that, so I had to trust it; I had to trust myself. Similarly, just as we find it hard to apply kindness to ourselves, we often find it difficult to trust ourselves. We would prefer someone else told us it's okay or a good decision. Learning to trust our own beliefs and decisions helps to calm all that negative Chatter down.

. . . And Back Yourself

Making that leap gave me the time and opportunity to turn my hand to writing, something I had wanted to try for years but never had the . . . well, guts to, and my books, *Happy* and *Calm*, grew from that space and vulnerability, but that's not to say that it was easy. There were huge moments of panic where I would lose all trust in my original plan and the Chatter would nostalgically remind me of what I had lost. I had meetings about the future with people I worked with where I was told my profile had weakened and my relevance to the masses over the years had been neatly arranged into a pie chart. I would get asked by friends of friends what I was up to or what I did for a living and had no real answer . . . 'I'm a um . . . bit of this, bit of that'.

Is there a decision that you need to make? Of course it's great to ask for advice from others, but could your gut instinct help you out here? To help you tap in to it, sit in a quiet place and stare at this all-knowing eye – think of it as your third eye. Give yourself at least five minutes and see if it can help you lock on to the answer and find a little quiet.

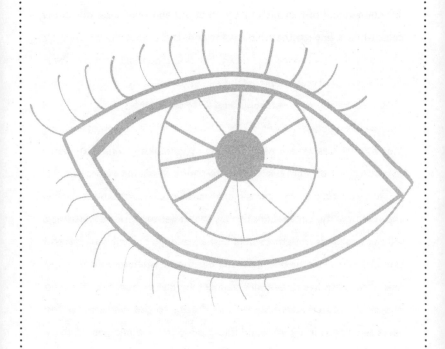

I didn't want to listen to the radio for a while as it felt too crushing not to be a part of it anymore, the FOMO Voice reminding me that I might never sit staring into Jared Leto's eyes again while quizzing him about his music, or lust over Haim's collective hair length in my cosy studio. All of these moments of change sparked up the mental Chatter. It grabbed hold of that pie chart with both hands and shoved it in my face, while telling me that this was the end. There would be no more TV shows, no more interviewing brilliant bands and no more creative flow.

I know a lot of mums feel that they slightly lose their own identity when they have a baby and I was somewhat experiencing this, with the added change of no actual job. Of course, what I have gained from having my kids is incomparable and the most shocking yet brilliant course of change I've been part of, yet it still presented some moments of professional uncertainty and concern. You may assume that, of course, I had a backup plan or someone who could sort this all out for me, but I really didn't. All I could do was trust that I would create enough change at some point and channel all of the energy that I had into something new. Trust, in this case, often has to be followed up by hard work and the willingness to start again, so that's what I did. I was back to square one with loads of ideas and a trust in myself that I could try something new.

Delving in to the world of mental health and well-being might have not been the obvious choice to the outsider but I knew it was something

I was deeply passionate about and something that was worth spending vast amounts of my time on. I knew it wouldn't be the quickest route yet deep down I found an inch of trust to hold on to as I moved in the right direction.

When making big decisions, we can of course sit and write up pros and cons lists and work out what rationally might be a good idea, but sometimes that won't be needed. Sometimes there will be a gut feeling that we know we should trust. It's almost inexplicable and I have experienced this on several occasions. Tapping in to our gut can sometimes feel very natural and easy and other times it is not. For us to really learn to trust our guts we have to quite literally find our quiet. I personally have to either go on a run, go for a walk in the fresh air without my phone, or sleep on it. Time, space and no noise to really root down to the answer that is already there. We can get so confused and bogged down by negativity and other regular thoughts that cloud the answer that's already there. A little quiet gives us the space and time to work out what we really feel and to trust it fully.

We don't need to think of trust, belief and hope as an exterior something that we must try to catch with a giant net, swooping haplessly though the air and sometimes missing; we can instead look within.

Trusting Again

How do we learn to trust again when we have been royally fucked over? I have been steamrollered into the ground by circumstance and other people so many times that it actually became tedious for a while back there. I'm not blaming or shunning my side of responsibility but whoever should take the flack, it happened a lot. I have been dumped, shat on by employers, replaced by others and also had a lot of well-laid plans fall by the wayside. I'm sure many of you have experienced this sort of rejection and upset, too. It's all part of life. Never nice, but as my friend Bonny puts it: 'All good fertiliser. If someone throws their shit at you, scoop it up and use it to grow.' As graphic as that analogy is, I love it! Wise, wise Bonny!

Picking yourself up in these moments can be excruciating as we feel ashamed, perhaps embarrassed and also very ruled by negativity. All of a sudden a narrative we weren't expecting defines us fully and we can't imagine how life will fix itself and start to tell a new story.

I think it's so important to mitigate the Chatter in these moments as fixing ourselves to one story can be so damaging. Those inner voices have the power to turn us from someone who was once dumped into someone who defines themselves as undatable. If we believe that negativity we can experience rejection at work and then enter a new workplace wearing that tag; 'rejected and probably not good enough'. If we let our Chatter take over, we can turn failure into future self-sabotage. There is such disproportion between reality and what that negative Chatter is telling us. Have a think now: is there a label that you have given yourself due to tough times? Have you told yourself and perhaps others that you are no good at finding a new job? That you are useless in social spaces? I do this all the time and I know it can hinder me greatly. I haven't driven on the motorway in some time as I had a series of bad panic attacks when zooming at 60mph. I heavily labelled myself as someone who cannot drive on the motorway. I'm now trying to make a concerted effort to trust in a different experience to what I have been through before. If I can get a little bit of quiet and step away from the exhausting inner dialogue, I can choose to remember that I have created this label for myself from a past experience. I don't have to be defined by it or suppressed by it in the future. I can be free of the Chatter if I step into the quiet and remember all of this. I can lock in to a quietness within that is cheerleading me on to trust in the future and other possible outcomes. It is my choice to either believe the events of the past define who I am today or to find some quiet and know that I can be courageous again.

I have gone through patches over the years where to feel hopeful

felt almost childish. I've had periods where I have viewed trusting in the positive as an extravagance I didn't deserve and I think that is quite a common train of thought for a lot of us. I guess it would be weird to be perpetually hopeful at all times and to consistently trust everything is going to be okay, as we are so used to seeing and reading about the dangers around us; it's hard to escape that in the modern world.

Yet sometimes we can find great strength in those moments of despair where we lose our faith and trust in everything. I know I have. I learned about humility and empathy in these moments and have taken a much closer look at other people going through tough times. Although it is perfectly normal to experience this I also think we have to be mindful as to how long we stay in that space. If we know we have wasted an opportunity or sabotaged a moment of good luck because we have forgotten how to trust in the future, then maybe it's time for change. Picking ourselves back up after failure or rejection isn't always easy but I think if we take it slow and start to place trust in the smaller things in life we can then build up to the bigger picture. Perhaps daring to trust in the little moments that create momentum, like smiling at strangers on your commute and trusting they'll smile back. Some might, some may not, but the ones that do will be enough to instill some positivity and trust in to your day. Maybe it's choosing to trust that even if you feel you've got a lot on your plate you'll seek out a little space and quiet among it all. Trusting in others or in yourself to make those tiny changes is a good opportunity to practise trusting in the bigger picture.

I think it's also important to look back at times when we felt beaten down yet still managed to dig deep enough to rise again, as we can then trust that it is possible in the future.

Within the outlines
of this rising phoenix,
write a list of times
you have risen again.

You Can Believe in it Until it's True

Sometimes if we really cannot find the strength to trust, we can turn again to that famous phrase 'fake it until you make it'. This plan of action doesn't need quite so much faith, you just need to sidestep the negative Chatter and self-doubt and just do the action bit. We don't even have to engage the gut and feel authentic self-belief, we just need to DO!

I have to engage with this way of thinking at work a fair bit as some days I do feel like crap due to being on my period/constipation/having had a row with Jesse. Nobody wants to hear me broadcasting on such matters, so I fake feeling positive until gradually I start to feel a bit better about it all. We can use this shortcut to get to the point where we can trust again. We may have been badly hurt by an ex-partner and feel we can't trust another again, but if we just jump in and get to the action bit of socialising with new people, we might just start to get that trust back step-by-step. If we have been sacked and have little trust in a better outcome in the future, we might just need to get back in to the driving seat with the action bit and let the mental side of things catch up later down the line. At times, we have to bypass the mind Chatter by just getting the ball rolling in a very physical way. You just start DOING, and eventually your mental patterns start to shift as you see the change you had been hoping for but had perhaps lost trust in.

It can be a cheesy old saying to knock about but having used it quite a lot over the years, I find it very helpful when needing to get off the start line. On your marks, get set . . . FAKE IT!

Letting Go

The other option is to LET GO!

Ah, I hate it when people (Jesse) tells me to LET GO!

'YOU let go, you wanker,' is my usual response.

My husband is annoyingly wise and almost always right so it irks me more than you might imagine. He is also the living breathing manifestation of this phrase so I can hardly ignore it as he is very much doing something right!

I am a control freak and so I DO need to let go almost all of the time. If trust cannot be located and my negative Chatter is telling me everything is going to shit the other option is to let go of it all. Let go of the tight grip I have on a particular outcome and let go of what I believe SHOULD happen and instead just stop. This isn't giving up or throwing in the towel, It's just having trust without admitting it. You're not focused on a purely positive outcome nor are you expecting imminent doom, you are just letting what needs to happen, happen.

This one I find the hardest because I'm determined. I'm like a little Jack Russell with a new toy I won't let go of. I can be feisty and don't like to give up or indeed let go. I sometimes view it as failure and let the mental Chatter take over, labelling me a flop! Yet really it is more often than not the exact thing I need to do, let go and just see what happens.

Letting go is 100 per cent about stepping in to the QUIET. One giant split leap into a space where you trust whatever is happening is perfect for you in that very moment. It's a quiet space as there is no brain Chatter – you surrendered to that the minute you stepped over the threshold. It's quiet because it is definite. You have committed to trusting in whatever is afoot and the lessons that may come from it. It's a silent surrender that could lead us to great personal expansion and growth. Yet there's usually great resistance from us know-it-all-humans to do so. Letting go is tough.

Sometimes trust can feel like a very loaded concept as we propose a fanfare of an outcome and then get disappointed when it doesn't work out that way. Letting go allows us to trust and feel grounded yet be open to any possible outcome. AKA my worst nightmare. I want the results I had envisaged to manifest and if they don't, I know my negativity will be immediately heightened and my confidence knocked. This is exactly why it is one of the most important lessons I personally need to learn.

I'm presented in life with many opportunities in which to practise this and often ignore them completely. Although I know letting go and trusting in what happens is the right way to go I try to force an outcome like a sweaty foot in an already too tight shoe. My adrenalin peaks, my Over-Congratulatory Voice sparks up telling me I know best and I get tunnel vision. What I should be doing is letting life unfold around me with the trust that whatever the outcome is, it'll be the right one for me. It might be a good outcome, a tough one or a mediocre one , but it'll be the RIGHT outcome for me to learn. It infuriates me that this is often the case and I can feel I'm actually punching the keys of my keyboard slightly more feverishly than normal right now as I battle against what I know deep down is true. Letting go is bloody hard but is perhaps our best option in trusting in the life that is yet to happen.

HELLO TO . . .
DUSTIN LANCE BLACK

In March of 2018, I approached Tom Daley and his husband Dustin Lance Black to see if they wanted to be on my podcast series, *Happy Place*. They had at this point announced that they were expecting a child via surrogate which opened them up for much public congratulation but also abuse. I found it completely absurd that anyone would find this happy moment a time to be discriminative or assuming so wanted to hear how Tom and Lance felt about it. Their interview was one of my favourites from the series as they are both so loving, wise and up for a debate on subjects they're passionate about. At the time of me writing this they have welcomed their little beautiful boy, Robbie, into the world and are loving parenthood and all it brings. I'm thrilled for them.

Lance's CV is not a short read. With an Oscar proudly displayed in their toilet at home in London for his work as a screenwriter and director, and huge respect for his constant and emphatic work in the LGBTQ community, he inspires many, me included. I touched on some of Lance's background in the podcast episode, but was intrigued about how he has mentally overcome much adversity in life and the courage it has taken to be an activist and public speaker. I'm not sure how, but in a blur of very new parenthood, he has managed to spill his heart out in this next chunk of the book and give a great perspective on courage and strength. This interview makes me weepy to read back on as I can almost feel his strength and passion bursting off the page. I hope you enjoy it as much as I have.

F: Lance, you are someone who has always had courage and used it well. Would you say your first courageous moment was coming out? How did that feel?

L: You are too sweet. Honestly, I haven't always had courage. I was a painfully shy child growing up. I didn't say more than two words outside of my home my first seven years of life. Courage is something I had to dig deep to find. I would say my first courageous moment arrived in a flash, when I was seven and out shopping for school clothes with my mom. I heard and saw what I might guess now was a 10-year-old boy, much larger than me, mocking my mother's braces, crutches, twisted spine and very different way of walking. My mom had been paralysed from polio since she was two years old and also suffered from polio-related scoliosis. She looked different. She walked different. But somewhere deep down inside of me, a developing sense of justice overtook my shyness on that day, and when my mom wasn't looking, I let that kid and his parents know how wrong his judgement was. I may or may not have also pinched the living hell out of the soft inside of his arm before running off, but I probably shouldn't be too proud of that last bit of Texas-style courage.

F: You're from an area of America that is known not to be tolerant of homosexuality. How did that affect the voices in your head and how you thought about yourself at that time?

L: I grew up in a Mormon, military home in San Antonio, Texas, in a family that hailed from Louisiana and Arkansas. Let's just say that the moment I knew I was a gay kid (about six years old), I already had a lot of names for what I was feeling (faggot, homo, pansy, queer) and none of them felt like words the wise would wish for. Mormons said I would be barred from heaven, the military said we weren't welcome, and most conservative states (like ours) still considered being gay a felony and a mental illness. That's a lot for a six-year-old to hold, and I didn't have a single voice in my life to counter their claims. So I believed them. And I started trying to hide, to disappear, to not excel or stick out. I didn't want to be caught. I wanted to be invisible. And that's what I did. I buried myself in shame, and I'd be lying if I said I didn't consider some very dire solutions to my circumstance.

F: Did you have a lot of negative Chatter at the time that told you that you shouldn't speak your truth and, if so, how did you combat that?

L: Where I grew up, homophobic Chatter sounded a heck of a lot more like it was coming out of a bullhorn. The Prophet of the Mormon Church was beamed into every congregation one fine Sunday via satellite, and he told all of us good Mormons that being gay was akin to murder. I also saw what happened to the boys with a certain flair who weren't as good at hiding as I was. They were mocked, derided and physically beaten. There was no way in hell I was going to speak my truth. Instead, I signed up for football and hid under my helmet. It was literally just too dangerous to speak the truth.

And do remember, this was the 1980s, there were no visible LGBTQ people in the media or in politics to draw inspiration from then. I thought I must have been the only boy like me in all of Texas or Mormondom. In that lonesome space, I bought the lie that I was wrong and damned.

My turn in life was thanks to a turn of luck that married up to a budding sense of justice. This turn of luck was my new Army stepdad getting orders to ship out to California. There, I began to realise there were other people like me, and that they didn't all have horns hidden under their hair like so many had taught me in Texas and in the church. That so many of the things that had been said about people like me were myths. And there, in a summer theatre programme, I would hear the story of an openly gay man who ran for public office and won. His name was Harvey Milk.

Just knowing that there was such a thing as an openly gay person, and that such a person might achieve, gave me hope, and from that hope, courage began to grow. That's the courage I would eventually use to come out myself, and then to marry to a growing sense of justice – drawn from a lifetime of watching my mom be judged for no good reason, the way she walked and looked – and within the next decade I would begin to fight for my larger LGBTQ family with my film and political work. Yes, that took courage, but it also took knowing that I wasn't alone, and a firm belief that injustice is a thing worth fighting to repair.

F: You seem to have channelled a lot of the feelings around sexuality and the discrimination around it into your films. Was that a cathartic process? Were you ever worried about the reaction to your work?

L: I tell stories related to my own experiences as an LGBTQ person because I think the best way to correct the record is to tell an emotional, compelling story. I believe that no matter how true and corroborative the statistics, law or science are to one's position, those arguments don't tend to change hearts, and I believe the only way to change a mind for good is to start with the heart.

I tell stories about my LGBTQ forefathers and foremothers because I know how much courage those stories would have given me when I was a boy back in Texas. If I had known people like me had existed for all of history, that we had achieved great things, lived full lives and that some had been fighting to help make my life better well before I was born, well, my entire childhood would have existed on a far higher plane. I want to keep giving that gift to future generations of children who are told they might be a bit too different for this reason or that. I want to help give them hope and courage to live their life with their magnificent differences held high.

As far as negative reactions and opinions go, those are none of my business. I have a job to do, and I do that job to the best of my ability – that alone is already hard enough work, so paying attention to others' reactions would only slow me down more. To be clear, this isn't something I've always practised. It's a practice that's come with time and experience. My mantra when times (and comments) get tough: 'Other people's opinions are none of my business.'

F: Your work as a very important LGBTQ activist has done so much good and has acted as a catalyst for much positive change. When you have to stand and talk in front of hundreds of thousands of people about something you're so passionate about how does it feel? Do you ever have self-doubt which holds you back?

L: I literally have to go to the restroom before any speech in front of more than three people. And like you said, I've given speeches in front of hundreds, thousands and even millions of people at this point. It's terrifying. It does, in fact, take courage for me to take the stage or step in front of the news cameras. Being very candid, I often feel a pang of doubt run through me just before it's go-time, whispering in my ear that I'm a fraud, that I'm a pretender, that I'm no true leader. And so, over the years, I've learned to confront those doubts with truth telling. If my greatest fear is that I'm a pretender, then I must get up in front of all of those people and just tell my truth as best I can. Because it's tough to screw up the truth. It's right there with you all of the time and you know it when you say it. That's my trick. And sometimes it changes hearts. Sometimes those hearts change minds. And those are the moments that make all of the potty breaks and sweaty collars worth it.

F: What is the greatest gain in your life that you know came from being courageous?

L: Helping to defeat Proposition 8 (which banned marriage equality in California, and became a symbol of US homophobic law), and in doing so, helping bring marriage equality to all 50 states. Yes, that gift was to gay and lesbian kids out there today who can now dream of getting married when they experience their first crushes, but it was also a gift to my childhood self. I now know without a doubt that with courage, dedication and wisdom, I can slay the dragons that tormented me as a boy. And that knowledge has made my courage grow stronger.

But of course, there is one even more personal, absolutely magical gift that sprang from my courage to come out, and I still can't believe this dream has come true: Tom and Robbie Ray. My family.

F: Crying again! Blinking heck, Lance, you are wonderful. Thank YOU!

Trusting in Others

When we are presented with fear and often pure evil on the news most days it can be hard to trust in the other humans that cohabit this tiny Earth with us. We see conflict and greed and reckless action which can quickly activate our Angry Voice. Feeling angry is of course A–OK if we channel that energy into making change we believe is beneficial, but just being angry for the sake of it or allowing that voice to infiltrate our minds is toxic all round. In these moments, we forget to trust at all. We create enemies and judge everyone around us, but, of course, it is so important to trust in others. To look out for the goodwill and support in the world, as well as witnessing the bad, otherwise we can quickly become so shut off and fearful of everything.

There are so many bright and beautiful souls on this planet and whenever I happen to stumble upon one in life my trust in humanity is fully restored – or at least recharged somewhat. We have to challenge the negative Chatter which tells us everyone is out to get us by trusting in others. It might not always work out, but once in a while we'll be surprised by the goodwill and generosity around us: that stranger who offers you their barely used parking ticket, the teenager your Self-Congratulatory Voice had labelled 'probably lazy' who just helped you carry your buggy down some stairs, the sweet lady who randomly complimented you on your new jazzy shirt when you were feeling a bit shit – let all of these moments restore your trust in the people around you. Our Chatter that is saying everybody is judging us or hating on us has to step aside to make way for these kind gestures and real life positivity, surely. When we start to look out for this good – well, it weirdly appears more and more frequently too. When we practise this sort of unexpected goodwill, we also become more open to believing in that trust as we see the ripple effects of its magic.

Trust is perhaps something we all need to practise daily. Don't mistake trust for making a wish and seeing it unfurl just as you had imagined, but perhaps instead a slight 'letting go', with the ability to observe what is happening all around. Trusting in where we are headed and trusting in ourselves will ultimately shun a lot of the negative Chatter as we route back to that gut feeling and what we truly know. More trust, less Chatter, more quiet!

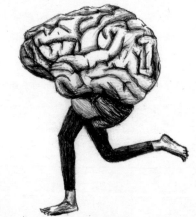

I can trust in the good, I CAN trust in change and I CAN trust in myself.

6

Quiet Sleep

The immediate relevance of this chapter when talking about mind Chatter might somewhat escape you, but bear with me, it's an important one. I am writing this chapter in a haze of sleep deprivation. A fog somewhat suffocating my mind, intercepting thoughts before they fully form. Unfortunately, a ubiquitous frame of mind at this point in my life. Sleep is a new currency in which I deal. Bartering with my husband, and longing for more of it, without knowing how to achieve such a feat.

Sleep? Yes, Please!

Some of you will fight against the necessity for sleep and push your own physical and mental boundaries by going out partying or staying up mega late watching TV. Others of you will have not much choice in how much or when you get it. Shift work, small kids or general life stress will alter and manipulate this much-needed respite whether we like it or not. I fit most definitely into the latter category for reasons I will explain in a minute. Whatever the reasons, the outcome of little sleep will always be the same. A foggy head, a physical funk which paves the way for more negativity and, hence, louder mental Chatter.

In my twenties, I couldn't have given a toss about sleep. It was the bit of the day when I wasn't striving for my personal goals or having fun. I would fly across the Atlantic regularly for work and exist in-between time zones in a coffee hyped-up state. I would occasionally drink alcohol on arrival to help me stay up later and then fall in to a deep intoxicated slumber that night, then drown in coffee the next morning in my new time zone to awaken my fuzzy head. I laughed in the face of jet lag on a weekly basis. I didn't give it much thought or worry about the effects at all. I might have to get up for work at 4 a.m. on some days yet on others have a day free with little responsibility, so could lie in a slumber until

10 a.m. It seems like a lifetime ago! So much fun but such a different lifestyle to the one I have today. HOW TIMES HAVE CHANGED!

These days, I can feel the anxiety of sleep rousing long before I hit the sack. I have weird routines and rituals that I believe will prepare me in the correct way to switch off and drift into a comforting blackness and keep the Catastrophising Voice at bay – the voice that will tell me at 2 a.m. that I might never sleep again. I turn my phone off around 9 p.m. so I'm not a slave to the blue light it omits so freely, I have a magnesium salt bath, spray my pillow with lavender-drenched sleep mist, rub lavender oil on my temples, try and clear my head and then surrender.

As you may have gathered from the previous 45,000-odd words, I'm not very good at surrendering or letting go. It is a low-level fear that everything will stop if I stop. Sleep requires this ultimate surrender. White flag waving to the day gone by no matter what has ensued. Perhaps preparing in such a ridiculous, meticulous and contrived way is actually part of the problem? Maybe the thought and worry around sleep is indeed the thing not allowing me to switch off?

HELLO TO . . . ROZANNE HAY

I met Rozanne through a friend after I had had my second child, Honey. I had gone back to work part-time at this point and already had a two-and-a-half-year-old so was keen to iron out a few sleep problems for the both of us. Rozanne is a child sleep specialist and she had such amazing advice during this time and her methods have helped me greatly. Who better to quiz on this subject and bring light to how sleep helps massively with our mental health and all the Chatter we hear.

F: You look at sleep rhythms and patterns in babies and the need for routine and consistency. Does the same thing ring true for adults?

R: All humans are regulated by the day and night cycles and the hormones they produce. Cortisol is what peps us up in the morning and a healthy balance of serotonin and melatonin prepare us for a good night's sleep. Any baby over four months will fully benefit from these natural rhythms which regulate our own circadian body clock, and the same holds true for adults.

Our bodies also take cues from light and darkness throughout the day, which contributes to a good night's sleep. It is important to wake up each day at a set time – and opening the curtains and/or switching on a bright light will set your day rhythms in motion. Taking a 20-minute walk outdoors during the mid-morning and late afternoon daylight is an excellent way to support your own circadian rhythms and will aid a restful night's sleep.

A winding down time is essential in preparing our body for sleep. This can be achieved by dimming lighting, avoiding screens and having a relaxing bath within the hour before bedtime. The warm water of a bath or shower trigger key biological and temperature changes in the body, which in turn release a flood of sleep hormones in anticipation of a good night's rest.

Each individual's sleep needs vary and a clue as to how many hours of sleep you need will depend on how you are feeling on waking in the morning.

F: If you're suffering from insomnia, is this usually linked to over-thinking?

R: There can be so many different reasons, from being overtired because you have an unpredictable daily work schedule, to anxiety disorders, sinus issues, having a new baby and many more reasons besides. If you're suffering from insomnia there are a range of behavioural support programmes that can help, especially Cognitive Behavioural Therapy (CBT-I). CBT-I has a high rate of success for insomnia sufferers as it enables them to reset their sleep patterns and gain control over their thought life.

F: What tips have you got for a good night's sleep?

R: To maximise our sleep potential we need a healthy balance of both the 'happy hormone', serotonin, in the day and the 'darkness hormone', melatonin, at night. Our 'peppy hormone', cortisol, which wakes us for the day, must function in sync with serotonin and melatonin in order to balance our 24-hour body clock. This is our 'circadian rhythm'.

We can support these hormones by controlling and co-operating with our environment, as I mentioned in my first answer above. Sometimes insomnia results when our minds are active at bedtime, so you may find it helpful to journal your thoughts – no later than about four hours before going to bed.

It's helpful to establish a set bedtime and waking time, although expect a period of adjustment when you move your bedtime earlier. It can take around five days for you to start benefiting from introducing a regular wake time and sleep time.

Other things you can try are switching off all electronic devices 90 minutes before bedtime, avoiding caffeine after lunch, getting a sound conditioner, sleeping with a weighted blanket and drinking banana peel or rooibos tea. Above all, it's ok if you are struggling to settle at night. Stressing over not being able to fall asleep only raises your stress levels further. It is better to get up and write in your journal, read a few pages of your book or make yourself a cup of herbal tea or warm milk and sit calmly in the darkness, rather than fretting and panicking about the next day's responsibilities.

F: What are the main causes of bad sleep in this day and age?

R: As a society, we are squeezing increasingly more into each day. Our working hours are steadily getting longer with less time for rest and recovery each week. Certain jobs lead to us having restricted sleeping hours and we often have unfinished work to complete at home before bedtime. We experience more stress than our bodies can handle and feelings of overwhelming helplessness result.

To add to the problem, as we age, our body produces lower levels of growth hormone. This can cause a decrease in melatonin production, with a reduction in slow wave, deep sleep. Consequently, we are likely to experience an increase in broken sleep. Around midlife and menopause, we experience additional hormonal changes which can create an imbalance. This imbalance can affect our ability to fall asleep or to remain asleep through the night. To overcome this, we can help our body tune into its natural rhythm by making sure we go to bed and wake up at the same time each day.

It's tempting to feel sleepy and nod off in the daytime. Make every effort to fight this daytime nap to ensure better sleep at night.

F: How much does environment affect sleep?

R: In your home, choosing lighting which corresponds with natural day and night rhythms is key to supporting our body's own circadian rhythms. When adjusting lighting in your bedroom, think of including sunset colours and shades such as orange, pink and red to incorporate in the winding down time.

There is mixed evidence surrounding the impact of blue light on the quality and duration of sleep. All electronic devices, including smartphones, TV screens and tablets emit a blue light which signals to our brains that it's mid-morning. These confusing messages we receive through the eyes, can disrupt our quality of sleep and ability to fall asleep. Although the research is not conclusive, it's a wise choice to switch off all screens well before bedtime.

F: How do bad sleep patterns or lack of sleep affect us mentally?

R: Many of us are all too familiar with the crippling emotions and inability to function after an overnight long-haul flight. Jet lag is a classic consequence of sleep deprivation. However, after a few good nights of sleep, we recover from such a loss of sleep.

But for people who experience this feeling on a daily or regular basis, especially over the long term, insomnia has a devastating effect on our ability to cope with decision making and impairs our executive function. Even the carrying out of menial tasks becomes overwhelming.

F: Thanks Rozanne – I'm off to paint my bedroom sunset orange immediately!

The Sleep Stealers

The reasons I may not sleep vary, but there are two main protagonists at the helm. The first is a red-headed three-year-old, who has a penchant for waking at 1 a.m. screaming that she wants to get up and start her day. And the second is our good old friend, negative Chatter. The red-headed, dream babe sleep thief is the easier to rectify as I can usually convince her to go back to sleep at some point, and even though she leaves me beyond tired with saggy eyes and hair like a bale of hay the following day, I know it's all beyond worth it. Her cherubim face staring back at me at 6 a.m. after a ropey night's sleep is a joy, no matter what.

Negative Chatter-fuelled insomnia, on the other hand, feels utterly pointless and thoroughly annoying. About two months ago, I had the worst sleep of my life and it was all down to my brain Chatter running away with itself. I had been through my usual, over the top pre-bed ritual and had taken even more care to ensure all was in place as I was covering for Chris Evans on the BBC Radio 2 breakfast show the following day. A prestigious job that I was really looking forward to, yet also slightly weighed down with the responsibility of doing it justice.

I slipped in between the sheets and tried my usual visualisation of inhaling one colour and then exhaling it before switching up the colour to repeat the same (a wonderful trick I learned from my wise friend, Yvonne, that usually works). After two hours of exhausting every Pantone on the colour spectrum, to the extent that at one point I consciously inhaled and exhaled Mole's Breath, which I believe is a Farrow & Ball paint colour, I started to panic. What if I didn't get to sleep until 1 or 2 a.m.? Then I would only get about four hours sleep! Disaster. Consequently, I would be shit on radio and never get asked back again.

'I'll maybe not even sleep at all now. Wait . . . WHAT! NO sleep at all? I'll go mad!' is how it started.

'But it's probably going to happen, so why don't I just get up now and do some emails or something rather than just lie here worrying about it all.'

I try to apply some common sense to the matter with, 'DO EMAILS? Are you mad?! I'll be wired and then feel deathly tomorrow when I'm on the radio. No, no I must sit this out and try to calm down again.' I tried so desperately to combat the negative Chatter with positivity and common sense, yet in the black and silence of the night, my Chatter felt so much louder.

I knew it was getting seriously out of control when my physical body started to listen to the Chatter. It believed every drama-drenched word and started to react accordingly. My heart quickened as if I was running on the spot. My lungs panted for breath and my eyes became large and very, very awake. Hellish. I then continued this nightmarish circle of events by worrying about the physical symptoms and panicking some more.

'Oh god, now I've really got things going. I'm a complete mess. Why am I not normal like everyone else who just simply goes to sleep? I will probably now be awful on the radio tomorrow so I guess I have good reason to panic.'

Which, in turn, made my body react further. A vortex of negativity and panic mentally and physically, all spurring on the Chatter.

In this moment, I really didn't know what to do. My usual toolkit of visualisations and techniques seemed obsolete and pointless. Luckily there was someone to talk to/panic about it with at this time. My husband got in from work late, around 1 a.m. so I spilled out tears of distress about how I may never sleep again. He is a very calming person so talked to me and my Chatter with a controlled and grounded voice. At 3 a.m., I eventually dropped off into a light wishy-washy sleep for two hours before my alarm shrieked out loud to alert me to the fact that I had to go and do a radio show to 10 million people without any rest. Luckily, due to experience and a bloody great team at Radio 2, I blagged my way through the show and actually really enjoyed every minute. Every concern and negative outcome dreamed up by my Catastrophising Voice was, of course, utterly not true. I didn't forget to introduce the news on the hour and I didn't freeze and forget how to use the radio desk; I merely felt a little groggy and had to concentrate slightly more than usual.

The Sleep Toolkit

This luckily isn't always the case when I cover on the radio or indeed do any new job that feels scary, but if I'm already overtired and feeling stretched, my sleep will be the first thing to go, which makes any Chatter that bit louder.

I wish I had a magic trick I could give any others out there to help with this torturous Chatter-led insomnia, yet there are some structures in life that I think help. If, like me, you feel overstretched at times and this messes with your REM then maybe look at delegating. I hate asking for help but know at times that if my plate is full I do need others to help me lighten the load. At least then I can flop onto the duvet each night knowing that most of my never-ending to-do list is under control. Ah yes lists . . . my total fave mental Chatter buster. I have three notepads on the go at any one time and I do find it very useful to spill out all worries, concerns, and odd jobs that need doing on to their pages before bed. Then there is no mental arithmetic or acrobatics needed through the night to keep them held in my memory. Also looking back at the previous chapter, a little trust is needed. Trust that you WILL fall asleep at some point. Trust that the next day won't be a complete write-off even if you don't. Trust that all will be well.

Then there are the physical tricks. I know that getting off my phone early in the day does work and having a magnesium salt bath does fill my body with heavenly lethargy most of the time. Keeping my gut healthy promotes a good night's kip too. I'm a big fan of kefir and try and treat my gut in the kindest way by avoiding refined sugars and processed foods. I discovered a goat milk kefir last year and it has been rather game-changing. It might taste like the hoof of a goat who has been rambling through a sewer but nonetheless the unsavoury taste is worth overlooking due to the health benefits all round. Aside from sleep, it helps with skin, energy and also makes that connection once again between our guts and minds. If we have an unhealthy gut, our heads will be impacted. This is something I only truly learned a few years ago. I thought that the food I ate had little to do with how I think and never did it cross my mind to think it would affect my sleep at all.

Have you ever eaten much later than you would normally like to and feel yourself tossing and turning in the night as you try desperately to digest this newly eaten food? Or chomped on some serious stodge before bed and then felt heavy and bloated and uncomfortable? Our bodies have to work extra hard to break down all of this newly eaten or heavy food, while it should just be concentrating on detoxifying and resting for the next day ahead. I have learned that eating light foods early makes me sleep much better. Due to dealing with insomnia on a regular basis, I know I can't eat anything too sweet before bed either. Once I ate a whole punnet of blueberries around 10 p.m. and then was wired until about 3 a.m. Never underestimate the power of the gut. Good gut health definitely helps with a dreamy night's sleep. That might sound mad as blueberries are healthy but I ate way too many and my body just wanted to party from all of the natural sugars.

If I'm really having trouble at night, when the brain Chatter is exceedingly loud, I will drown it out with someone else's voice. A guided sleep meditation online, where someone else's bold and true words guide me into a night's sleep so I can block out the mental Chatter.

On the occasions like the one before I covered Chris Evans' show, when none of the above is helping and where this pattern is going on for a few nights, I will go and seek out some reflexology. There's a brilliant and inexpensive place near me that I'll pop to before bed if I can so someone can work their magic on my feet. I'm not an extravagant person but this hour of foot-rubbing heaven really makes me happy. Not only do I really enjoy the experience but it helps with my sleep so much. Each point in our feet correlates directly with other areas of the body so a little diagnosis is available after a session as well as remedy. I find it completely miraculous and beyond enjoyable. It's making me feel sleepy just thinking about it now.

When Routine Isn't Possible

My lovely wind-down routine is usually very helpful, but as my work is sporadic, sometimes I will have to film in to the evening, so my wind-down time is cut very short. In these situations, the night-time Chatter can get lively. It will perhaps pick apart all I have recorded that day or sometimes weirdly just replay the whole day's events on loop in my head with a running commentary. Do you ever experience a heightened mental Chatter if you've had a late night or are out of routine? It all feels rather annoying and pointless to have to listen to this Chatter on loop when you'd rather be asleep. In these moments, again I will reach for my earphones and plug them into my phone and find an online meditation on YouTube. In desperate times, I just need the soothing voice of another to help block out my own Chatter.

The hangover to a bad night's sleep is that sometimes the negativity continues at a heightened volume the following day. Problems and worries that seemed manageable the previous day become insurmountable and fluorescent in colour. Self-doubt and self-loathing are inflated for no particular reason, the mental Chatter again reinforcing every fault and mishap. Today I am tired so I am feeling all of this. Perhaps not an ideal time to sit and try and write a book! But also maybe the perfect time, as I am dealing with all of these emotions currently:

I have had my negative Chatter telling me I should feel guilty for writing while my daughter is at nursery.

I have had it squeal that I must not stop or slow down otherwise I'll fall behind.

I have had it shriek that I am not good enough and should be consumed with worry and fear.

I don't know the reason behind all of this unnecessary and volatile stuff but I do know why I am hearing it. Because I haven't had enough sleep.

I have to, in these moments, go back to basics and remember that none of it is true and I'm only hearing all of this bollocks in my head because I'm tired. My concentration is off, my thoughts are slightly warped and I need to rest. A warning sign that I must listen to much more than the dialogue from the Chatter!

Finding our quiet in these moments is so important so we can reduce

the damage and stop ourselves from getting even more tired. Maybe it's a slow walk out in the fresh air or a peaceful read of a feel-good book on our lunch break. We have to go easy on ourselves and not push through the tiredness, as that's when we get ill. Physically and mentally, it'll all take its toll if we don't rest, and once again I have learned this lesson the hard way. Of course, we'll all sleep better if we are more rested, too. I have learned this from my kids. An overtired kid rarely sleeps well whereas a rested one who has had a nap earlier will drift off to the land of nod with ease.

Don't Let Panic Win

What I'm personally working on at the moment is reprogramming my mind to not panic when I can't sleep. When I was younger, sleep was just something that marked the end of one day and the start of another, so I know I CAN do it. Replacing negative thought patterns around any circumstance in life, no matter how banal, takes discipline and an open mind and this is something I very much need to practise every day. I have to find the balance between combatting the pre-sleep Chatter by replacing negative thoughts with positive mantras yet also trying to let go and not overthink it. What a balancing act, yet I know I need to let go and dead-end the panic before the inner narrative takes hold and blows it up into something much bigger. I will practise this one today. I had a shitty night's sleep last night but tonight could be different. It could be the best night's sleep ever. It also might not be and that's okay, too. If it is not I will be kind to myself tomorrow and take it easy rather than berate and curse myself for having let the Chatter win.

Reading Your Dreams

The other interesting thing about the night-time and how our inner voices work is, of course, how our dreams manifest. I love grabbing hold of loose memories on awakening and trying to piece together the visuals to the feelings I was experiencing when asleep. The caveat to the joy of dreams being the exhausting tedium of having to listen to another person's.

'Hey Fearne, wanna hear about my dream last night, my god it was mental! I was canoeing with Ryan Gosling and then a giant goat jumped out of the water and . . . '

Oh god, I DON'T CARE! It wasn't real and also it didn't happen to me! Dreams are wonderfully self-indulgent – and should possibly remain that way. They can be super interesting to privately mull over though. They are the space and quiet that connects the dots between our reality and complete fantasy. The part of our lives where our brains can cavort off in any direction as they try to process the previous events and the feelings around them. There is no self-editing or even reason, just millions of thoughts and images appearing like a Dalí-esque seven- or eight-hour-long movie.

Our dreams can also help us distinguish which voices within our own negative Chatter spectrum are getting the limelight. Do you ever have anxiety dreams about an upcoming situation you're nervous about? A recurring dream (and I'll keep this brief as I know how dull this could get for you!) of mine always shows up when I'm about to cover someone else's show on the radio. The dream is always the same. I'm at a radio desk and on the air; as I reach to fade up my microphone I realise that it is about two metres away from me. I dash over to use it only to realise the next button I need to touch is a whopping two metres to the other side of the desk. Nothing works! The buttons I'm pressing seem to have shut down, along with my ability to explain to the nation what the hell is going on. I can clearly see that the Catastrophising Voice is heavily at work ramping me up for a huge shot of adrenalin and nerves the next day. Knowing this allows me to remember that I may have a little anxiety around the job, yet the dreamed-up outcome is purely fantasy and steered by the negative Catastrophiser!

On other occasions, I'll dream of a house. The building will change in look and feel, but the one element that remains the same is the discovery of new rooms. I'll open a door to a house I have supposedly been living in for years only to discover a huge attic with tonnes of space and potential. The feelings are of excitement and discovery: I know when I wake up that I am perhaps about to learn something new or am open to new situations in life. I can see that the mind Chatter has taken a bit of a back seat and that I'm in a good and open state.

I also have a fair few dreams about Dave Grohl, but I'm not sure they have much relevance or bearing on my mental Chatter or fate. Shame! (PS: my husband will never get this far into the book to read this information!)

HELLO TO . . . CLARE JOHNSON

I'm so intrigued as to what our dreams mean and why we have them in the first place, so I started searching for someone to answer my many questions on the matter when writing this book. Dr Clare Johnson is President of the International Association for the Study of Dreams, and the author of several books, including *Dream Therapy: Dream your way to health and happiness*. Her website is packed with information about lucid dreaming and she responds to questions on any aspect of dreams, nightmares, and sleep disturbances here: www.DeepLucidDreaming. com. Clare very kindly took some time out to delve a little deeper into the land of dreams.

F: Does everybody dream?

C: Everybody dreams every night. The average person has around six dreams a night, or 2,000 dreams a year. We spend nearly six entire years of our lives dreaming. Imagine how much of life we miss out on when we don't remember our dreams! Luckily, it's easy to get into the habit of recalling dreams, and our dreaming mind responds when we show an interest in our dreams.

F: What is going on in our heads when we dream? Are we processing information from previous moments and our day just gone, or is it a matter of our brains going off without control as we are asleep?

C: Some people used to believe that dreams were the result of random neurons firing in the brain while we sleep, but modern neuroscience shows that dreams help us to lay down long-term memories and help the learning process. Scientific studies show that dreams have a problem-solving function and help us to experiment with creative solutions. Dreams also have a healing function: they can flag up illness and disease in the body, and each night they release too-strong emotions and help us to process life events. Dreams emerge from our unconscious and I think of them as 'inner movies': in a stream of vivid imagery, they tell us stories about where we are in our lives right now, what our relationships with others are like, and how we really feel deep inside. This is why it's so exciting – and so important – to pay attention to our dreams!

F: If we remember our dreams does that mean we have slept well?

C: Dreaming is a healthy part of sleep, but no, remembering our dreams doesn't always indicate that we've had a restful night of sleep. Not all dreams are pleasant, and some people find their sleep is beset with dreams which have high levels of anxiety or fear. Others have wake-up-screaming nightmares! But I always say that nightmares (however horrible) are healing gifts, because the role of bad dreams and nightmares is to flag up an emotional issue that we need to pay attention to and resolve in order to stay healthy and happy.

F: If we don't remember our dreams is that due to light sleep?

C: Light sleep is more likely to result in good dream recall; it's the deep sleepers who have more trouble remembering what they got up to in the night. This is because in the lighter stages of sleep, we are more mentally alert, and this is the sleep stage associated with rapid eye movement sleep (REM), when the brain is extremely active and we find ourselves having vivid, bizarre, emotional, film-like dreams, like sailing over the edge of a waterfall, or giving an impassioned speech only to look down and realise we are stark naked . . . exactly the kind of dream that sticks in the mind!

F: Why are dreams so hard to recall in detail the next day?

C: We've all had that dismaying feeling of a vivid dream slipping elusively from our grasp when the alarm clock goes off or the family dog leaps on us first thing in the morning. This is because the moment we allow thoughts of the day to come to intrude, our brain switches gears and enters 'day mode'; we remember our 9 a.m. meeting, or wonder what the weather's like, or remind ourselves to buy cat food. The moment we do this, our dreams seem doomed to recede from our consciousness, and unless we take care to retrieve them, within minutes (or even seconds) they've vanished. But as with so many things in life, recalling dreams is a question of habit.

F: What are your best tips for learning to recall dreams?

C: The best way to improve your dream recall starting from tomorrow morning is to set a clear intention that you will remember your dreams and say it like a mantra before you sleep and whenever you wake up briefly in the night: 'I will remember my dreams!' Also, avoid using an alarm clock if possible, or use a musical one that starts with a mellow song that you love. When you wake up, don't open your eyes immediately and don't move from your position, just think back and ask yourself, what was I just doing? How was I feeling? Who was I with? Even if all you can remember is a colour or an emotion, write it down. As you keep practising, you'll remember more and more detail and you should soon start to remember entire dreams.

F: Is it useful to keep a dream journal?

C: Absolutely – this sends a strong signal to our dreaming mind that we are interested in connecting with it – and dreams respond to attention like flowers to sunlight. When we write down our dreams, we start to discover which themes come up most often for us, which emotions dominate, and we become familiar with our own symbolic language. It's good to write down dreams in the present tense, as this draws us into the scene and improves our recall. Keeping a dream journal is also a powerful step towards becoming lucid in our dreams – which is when we realise that we are dreaming, while we are dreaming, and can guide the dream if we want to.

F: Should we take notice of the information presented to us in dream form? If we feel they may have given us a sign or a nudge in a particular direction?

C: Yes, if we feel our dreams are pointing out a particular direction to take, it's a good idea to pay attention to this. Dreams can be pretty persistent when need be and they may recur until we get the message. The thing to remember is that all dreams come to help and heal us, no matter how baffling, scary, or downright odd they can sometimes appear to be! When we work with dreams and nightmares to unwrap their meaning, we are doing important psychological work, a kind of self-therapy (or Dream Therapy, as I call it), to understand and change deep-rooted negative psychological patterns that are present in our lives and that can cause long-term unhappiness until we wise up to them and take steps to move on from them.

F: What can we learn from our dreams and how can we apply that information to life?

C: Having worked with dreams for most of my life, I think it's safe to say that dreams can help us with any aspect of life. They can help us through loss and bereavement (dreams of deceased loved ones can be remarkably healing), they can give us creative ideas, they can help us to become more compassionate towards ourselves and others because they teach us empathy by showing us how we – or other people – really feel about a situation. Dreams can give us insight into physical illness or psychological malaise, and they can also give us a much-needed slice of pure fun and happiness, because they can be joyful, sensual, and refreshing. We can work through trauma by doing dreamwork, and create a nourishing, healthy communication between our conscious and unconscious mind. Dreams help us to find solutions to dilemmas, and give us strength when we're experiencing disaster in our lives. When we wake up to our dreams, we wake up to our deeper, wiser self. We unlock our potential and are empowered to take action to create a happier, more authentic life.

F: Often fears and anxiety manifest in dramatic or strange ways in our dreams. If we are calmer in life and have more control over stress do these dreams lessen?

C: It works both ways. It's good to calm down in waking life, but it's also important to work on the deeper level of dreams to cause lasting change. We're not separate from our dreams – far from it. Our dreams act as mirrors showing us what is really, honestly going on with us. It can be so easy to separate ourselves from our true feelings and lose touch with who we are on the deepest level. When we engage mindfully with our dreams by recalling them, writing them down, and working with them in simple ways to unwrap their message, we create powerful change on the unconscious level. This change quickly manifests in our waking life in the form of positive change.

The way I see it, the best approach is to become more mindful on both the 'conscious' and 'unconscious' levels. When we view waking life and sleep and dreaming as equally valid aspects of human conscious experience (instead of viewing waking life as the only important part), we enable calm awareness and joy to fill each of these aspects of life. The transformation and healing that then arises can be remarkable and life-changing.

CLARE'S DREAM INDEX

What does it mean when we dream of . . .

F: Flying. I have this one a lot. Sometimes hovering a metre from the ground in a front crawl swimming style and at other times way above my house.

C: First off, although some dreams have common themes, it's wise to avoid the temptation of slapping one meaning onto these, as so much depends on the emotions of the dreamer, their personal life experience, and their individual associations with the imagery. It's more useful to unwrap the dream by asking yourself a few questions about it or doing simple dreamwork exercises (such as the ones in my book, *Dream Therapy*) to discover what your dream is saying to you.

Whenever you dream about anything, it's really useful to identify the main emotions, as these provide a clue to its meaning. Some people have thrilling flying dreams where they swoop effortlessly through the sky feeling alive and happy, whereas others have frustrating flying dreams where they can't seem to get off the ground properly, or crash into something, or feel terrified as they gain height. Happy flying dreams might be taken as a reflection of your feelings of confidence or delight in a current life situation. If you have a flying dream where you simply can't fly despite all your efforts, this may reflect a project in your life that you're having difficulty 'getting off the ground'. Flying dreams can also be associated with sexual or creative energy. A key question to ask yourself after any dream is: 'When did I last feel this way in my waking life?' Often, you'll then instantly understand which situation is being referenced in your dream.

F: Losing teeth. This always seems to be a common one?

C: We've all had the actual experience of losing a mouthful of teeth as we grew up and our milk teeth fell out, but it's still quite dismaying when your teeth fall out in a dream! A dream of losing teeth may be linked to feelings of insecurity, instability, life changes, and loss. It can also be linked to a sense that we've reached a stage when we can no longer hide how we really feel – we can't smile and pretend all is well, because we have no teeth to smile with! If you have this dream, ask yourself: 'Am I doing what I really want to do with my life?' If the answer is 'no', it may be time for a change.

F: Walking around your local home town with no clothes on. This is again a recurring one for me.

C: These 'naked in public' dreams are really common. Much depends on how you feel in the dream when you discover your nudity. Are you horrified? Do you try to cover yourself up? Do you feel exposed and embarrassed? Or are you walking jauntily down the street butt-naked feeling confident and relaxed? Naked-in-public dreams might point to a feeling of over-exposure or vulnerability in a current life situation or relationship, or they might be a strong affirmation that you are saying to the world: 'This is who I am! I'm happy with myself, warts and all!' Only you, as the dreamer of this dream, can unwrap the true message here. One easy dreamwork technique to help with this would be to imagine yourself back in the dream at the moment you realise you're naked and then speak with the voice of your dreaming self, starting with the words, 'I feel . . . '

F: Being on stage with a band, holding a guitar yet with no knowledge of how to play the instrument.

C: This dream has many variations – my own is when I find myself sitting in an examination hall but when I turn the exam paper over, my stomach drops to my boots as I realise I haven't revised at all! Such dreams tend to show that we feel unprepared on some level. But how much is this unpreparedness bothering us? Look at the feelings in the dream to find out. When you're on stage holding that guitar, do you feel anxious about not knowing how to play? Or are you unfazed? Identify the feeling, then make a bridge to a waking-life situation where you feel the same way. Often, dreams show us how we really feel about something, and once we've acknowledged this inner feeling by identifying the message of the dream, we can then act to help ourselves. Whenever I get my exam dream, I ask myself what's on the horizon that I may be feeling 'not ready' for, and then I make a point of preparing thoroughly for that interview I'll be giving, or the meeting I'll be chairing.

F: Do specific animals have meanings e.g. a snake? A spider?

C: Animals have meanings specific to the dreamer, because our associations with animals are so different. A dream cow won't have the same meaning for a British butcher as it does for someone from India, where cows are viewed as sacred. Dream animals are fascinating as they often represent our hidden instincts and energies, our inner power. When you dream of an animal, try this simple exercise to discover what it means: imaginatively become the animal in your dream and see the world through its eyes, then write without stopping to think or judge, beginning with the words: 'I am . . . ' This writing technique can bring surprising insights, and it can work with any element of the dream; objects, people, landscapes or animals, can each represent different aspects of ourselves.

F: My most recurring dream is where I am in a house that I know belongs to me, yet I open a new door I hadn't seen before and it leads on to several huge new rooms that are yet to be explored. It's an exciting dream which I enjoy having.

C: What a wonderful dream, Fearne. This is also a common one, and if it's accompanied by feelings of excitement, it tends to reflect a journey of personal discovery; this might be intellectual discovery, or the beginning of a friendship, sexual exploration, or a new creative phase. It's a dream of magical potential!

F: Having sex with a friend. Always mortifying when you have to see them the day after!

C: Sex dreams are so interesting, partly because most people don't realise that sex dreams are not always about sex! When we dream of having sex with someone we know, this could just mean that they possess some quality that we feel we need more of, such as high self-esteem, the ability to make friends quickly, or vibrant health. It's never worth beating yourself (or your partner!) up about a sex dream – even when you have a disturbing one.

A very common sex dream is one where we dream our partner is having hot sex with somebody else. We may wake up feeling betrayed or even suspicious. But mostly, such dreams don't point to a literal infidelity. People in our dreams may symbolise an aspect of ourselves. If you dream of infidelity, ask yourself: 'Am I being untrue to myself in some way?' This type of dream may reflect a feeling about life, so you could ask yourself: 'Where in my life do I feel cheated?' If you feel the dream is related to your partner, ask yourself: 'Do I feel unsupported by my partner? Are we happy together? Do we need to change anything about our relationship?'

Re-enter your dream imaginatively and interview your cheating partner or the platonic friend/unattractive co-worker you had dream sex with. Ask him or her: 'What do you want to say to me? Why are you in my dream?' This dream interview technique can result in powerful insights. When we engage with our dreams through simple dreamwork, we quickly reach the heart of the dream.

F: Thank you Clare that was so fascinating! Dream on dreamers!

My Dream Diary

Over the next week, as soon as you wake up jot down any dreams you had during the night. Then see if any of your dreams relate to the ones Clare has explained.

MONDAY	
TUESDAY	
WEDNESDAY	
THURSDAY	
FRIDAY	
SATURDAY	
SUNDAY	

This chapter has very much been an ode to sleep. For years, I failed to look at its significance and/or have the respect I have for it now. If you don't feel the need to be too bothered about it right now, just remember how important having enough of it is to keeping your mental Chatter in check.

More sleep and rest equals less Chatter and more QUIET in life. We so often see 'Living my best life' typed underneath photos on Instagram of people partying the night away. Well, my best life these days involves an eye mask and a TEMPUR® pillow.

I know good sleep will lead to less Chatter and more quiet. I know less Chatter and more quiet will lead to good sleep.

7

Quiet and Still

I am scared of being still. It is perhaps my biggest fear.
Bigger than the terror I feel when an eight-legged fiend is
in sight. Larger than when I'm looking over a balcony
10 storeys up. More overpowering than when I know
embarrassment is looming. Deep down, feeling scared of
being still is my greatest driving force to do good yet my
worst enemy all rolled in to one.

On the Run

I fidget, keep on the move, one eye on the goal ahead, the other scouting around for my next step. I look, hear, react, do, run, type, talk, write. I cannot stop. I am one of those annoying people that spring out of bed and glug a coffee ready to take the day on with a pen and checklist in hand. I usually feel excitement for the work ahead, whether it be career-based or more domestic. I like cleaning my home, I love keeping on top of the shopping and things we need as a family, I love writing and emailing people I know may have some interesting thoughts or connections to the work I'm concentrating on. I feel almost high when I'm doing it.

Now I know there is nothing massively wrong with this and actually I'm rather lucky to have this energy and drive, but I'm not backing it up with the rest and rejuvenation I probably mentally and physically need – something we established in the last chapter is a complete necessity for quiet. I convince myself that I don't need to take a break or have a day where I do very little.

As I have said, I'm not fussy about what the 'doing' bit involves. It can be banal and tedious like the washing up as long as I feel I'm doing something. Some of this lies in feeling a sense of purpose. When I cook

for my children, or sit and read with them, I know that my doing so is part of a bigger picture. I am partly on this Earth to teach them what I can and guide them in the way I deem appropriate. When I do a good job at work, or write an article that I feel may resonate with others, I feel that my purpose has been fulfilled and that my energy and drive were simply connecting with this potential. Yet a lot of the doing I do cannot be filed under this heading. A lot of my doing is simply for the sake of it – to cover my fear of stopping with a giant unhelpful plaster.

My mental Chatter told me only moments ago that although Honey and Rex are at nursery/school and I still have two hours until the school run, I mustn't sit in the sunshine in the garden on the hottest day of the year as that would be lazy and unnecessary. It tells me I must continue and not stop and not lose focus. This internal pushing has led me to take a closer look at why and to try and unearth what is really afoot.

I have come to two personal conclusions as to why I am so shit scared of stopping:

Conclusion one: I don't feel good enough.

How many of you feel this way? How many of you are driven because inside you don't feel enough? I'm sure many of you will be nodding along to this section of the book. There is no discrimination with this one. You can be super successful, top of the class, the most popular, the most copied or praised and you'll possibly still have this sense of lacking inside. Even though my negative Chatter was telling me I couldn't stop and sit for 30 minutes in-between writing sessions an hour or so ago, I bucked against this onslaught and sat peacefully and quietly in the sun. I let the feelings that were swirling around and firing up the Chatter rise to the surface rather than suppress them back down with chores or the need to 'do'.

At first, the emotions felt confused and muddled but quite quickly I realised that beneath the doing was a huge sense that I am not enough. Now, if I break this down I have to strip myself away from the titles I've given myself within my working life, the tag of being a mother, a wife, a friend and the history that has led me to learn and explore. Who is the person beneath all of these social tags? And why isn't she enough? Why is it so bad for me to simply be? Why do I have to have accolades and achievements to feel okay?

I'm not talking about the feeling of elation here, simply just okay and, I guess, safe? Why do so many of us feel scared without actual danger afoot? Most of us are scrabbling for a feeling of safety subconsciously without really knowing why.

Again I could point a finger at society for the fact that most women are subliminally told they're not enough so that we buy the latest eye cream, shoes or spa treatment. I could blame pop culture and the way that women are portrayed to be desired and sexual to gain attention. I could look at how we confuse social media with reality and compare ourselves to so many we really don't know. But maybe, just maybe it's none of that.

Perhaps I need to point the finger at myself and know that I have been listening to the negativity inside me far more than I should have been and need to give myself a break and talk to myself in a much kinder way? Perhaps I can personally only do this in the stillness that drags me away from my constant need to 'do'.

It feels uncomfortable for me to sit there in stillness just being. I physically find myself reaching for a phone to scroll through to give my brain something to dissect and talk about. I find myself writing mental lists of things I need to do. Have I, perhaps, in my older age forgotten how to daydream? I used to be the queen of daydreaming. I swear that's how I made all this career stuff happen. I used to daydream more than I was awake to what was going on around me. I would be sat in an English lesson at school and while my teacher was giving us the ins and outs of *Lord of the Flies*, I would have drifted off to a film premier in Cannes with Leonardo DiCaprio, while wearing an exquisite gown rather than an itchy, grey school skirt. I dreamed my way into my career as my visualisations were so lucid. I was very good at just being and letting my mind wander without the constant need to do.

I am making a concerted effort to drift off mentally a lot more than I have been this past decade. No phone in hand, no distractions, no self-judgement, just letting thoughts bubble up freely. Again I think practice might help me with getting back in to the swing of it. Replacing all of those lists and 'must do's' with a blissful break of nothingness. A big chunk of quiet. I have to also connect with the part of me, again more than likely my gut, which knows I am enough. Without the tags and achievements or ability to get loads done; that simply being me is okay.

Conclusion two: the terror of what else might pop up mentally if I let my mind go blank.

I know there may be some self-doubt lurking as I've just explained, but what else might I have to sit with? The memory of something thoroughly embarrassing that took place 10 years ago? The knowledge that I could have chosen a different path in my twenties and avoided a lot of drama? The feeling of regret wrapping itself around every bone? I'm scared that only the negative will loop around my mind and that I'll somehow have to make peace with it all or find a way of resolving a lot of what has been or is subsequently on the horizon. So instead I push through all of that debris in my mind and replace it with automated instructions to complete tasks. I walk away from the mess and worry by completing lists and creating new work and chores for myself. If I keep moving, maybe it'll be okay. If I rush a little more, maybe my speed and haste will overtake all of this stuff chasing me.

Again, what if I just sat, in stillness and silence and let all of that shit rise to the surface? What would really happen? It might feel uncomfortable and irksome but maybe then I could indeed start to reason with how the Chatter presents these memories and this information to me. Maybe I could put some of these concerns to bed for good? Maybe I could talk to another about some of it rather than pushing it all under a giant rug of shame? Maybe it wouldn't be so bad after all.

Anything that is habitual and practised often is hard to break free from. As I'm addicted to and obsessed in doing, I need to learn to get into the groove of the opposite every now and then.

If I actually do stop and stuff floats up to the surface like debris from a shipwreck, it might feel painful but maybe over time and with a little practice I will be able to actually resolve some of these fears and worries so that next time they pop up I'll fell that bit stronger in dealing with them.

When I have had those moments of stillness, whether it felt comfortable at first or not, a funny thing has happened; for those of you that meditate regularly or are naturally good at resting, you'll think this to be exceedingly obvious, but I have gained such clarity. It may take a while or three of four attempts but in such moments of stillness I do eventually manage to lose the negative voices altogether. They start to sound quieter, as if in the next room, and their mutterings seem almost comical rather than serious and alarming. I can still hear the dialogue and thoughts will still pop into my head but I let them go again, quite quickly remembering they're not important or needed in this moment. Eventually, I find that my head has stopped dreaming up quite so many worries and I'm not berating myself for the past so much and I'm a little more focused on what is happening around me rather than what is whizzing through my brain. Stillness can seem exposing with its lack of action as we often become more focused on what is going on in our minds, but if we pull focus from our thoughts and concentrate on what is around us and how our bodies feel, the voices start to lose their grip. We settle in to this quiet and with practice this can be a great tool to use when we know the negative Chatter has gotten out of control.

What jobs or activities do you know stop you from sitting with certain feelings or memories? Write a list of all the DOING you do to suppress the feelings and then next to them write down what feelings you're afraid will pop up and why.

....

....

....

....

....

....

....

....

....

....

....

....

....

The Wonder of Space

These moments of stillness don't have to offer up greatness, inspiration or euphoria, they offer something far more beneficial; space. Something we all lack massively in this day and age as we are constantly bombarded with information, news, other people's views and more and more to digest mentally. Stillness can offer us space and slow down time. Maybe within that space and quiet we will experience calm or a sense that we are, indeed, enough.

Do you ever invite chaos and drama into your life? Is that your habitual pattern stopping you from, well . . . stopping?

It can be a hard thing to admit but some of you may be addicted to drama and don't quite know how to live without it. I think I used to be like that, to some extent, and can still be lured occasionally by drama today. In my twenties, I would invite a little chaos into the mix to test myself to see how I would react. I most definitely avoid it these days as best I can as I know that I work best as a parent, wife, friend and creative in very calm and undramatic circumstances. Of course, some drama is unavoidable and we cannot predict its arrival so there is a big difference there. Only we will know when we have invited drama in by initiating confrontation and dilemma vs the unexpected that we really didn't ask for. If you have or indeed regularly do bring drama into your life, how would you feel without it? Does the stillness or calm scare you, perhaps? If so, why? Only you will know the answer but it is good to explore the 'why' as it helps us to ensure we are making the right decisions for ourselves.

Banish Unwanted Drama

Sometimes there are people in our lives we feel very strongly about. We know they don't agree with us or our lifestyles or their behaviour irks us somewhat, yet we still allow our negative Chatter to talk about them, constantly stirring up drama and the unwanted circumstance of having them in our lives. We stop stillness and peace entering the scene as we become tunnel-visioned and only allow negative Chatter in to enlarge their importance in our lives. This is one very easy way to let drama in. My husband always says 'get them off your bus'. You imagine asking them to get off of the metaphorical bus that you are the driver of and then close the doors behind them. I have to admit on occasions I have visualised drop-kicking some off my bus in an almost cartoon-style manner. Whatever it takes, get them off your bus and let the stillness ensue.

Sometimes stillness can be enforced and very unwanted but perhaps even in the most awful situations this static can bring a little chink of calm or perspective and that is worth grabbing hold of. When we get sick – or, in my case, nine months of near debilitating pregnancy (it's the only thing I have in common with the delicious Kate Middleton, terrible, terrible sickness) – everything has to slow down as there is no choice in the matter. Sometimes a new pace of life can be adjusted to and we can then gain a new perspective – a much-needed piece of quiet.

HELLO TO . . . JO WOOD

My husband's stepmother, Jo Wood, AKA Granny Jo, has recently had a life-changing trip courtesy of the one and only Bear Grylls. She was dropped off in the middle of the North Pacific Ocean to survive for 28 days without any of the usual basics one would need to survive. When Jo first called to tell us she had signed up for this total lunacy, I instantly knew she would be completely fine. She is perhaps one of the few people I know that has iron-like mental strength. She is able to battle through stress and sticky situations with a smile on her face and she naturally has a strong constitution for mental upheaval. I'm happy to say that I was proved completely right as she not only lasted the full month stranded in the middle of nowhere, but actually enjoyed a lot of it, too. With her new group of island mates, she had to keep a fire alight for the duration of the trip, forage for whatever food might be available and sleep on a hard bed of nothing but sand. She, of course, became a matriarchal figure to the team, making broth out of fish remains and keeping the mood lifted with her spirit. We all need to be a bit more like Jo at times. I think I would have lasted about two days before screaming in Bear Grylls' face to get me off the island. We had an amazing chat about this experience on her return and I loved hearing about the peace and solitude she found in the simplest of moments, so who better to talk to in this chapter about STILLNESS. She had 28 days of the good stuff, so let's find out more.

F: How much negative mental Chatter do you normally hear?

J: I don't think I ever really hear negative mental Chatter. If I'm doing something I'm nervous of, I'll remind myself of things I've done in my life and say, 'come on Jo, you can do this'. Or if I'm not feeling positive about something, I say, 'positive thinking, Jo, positive thinking'.

F: I'm so in awe of your life-changing trip to a deserted island with no luxuries and just the need to survive. I loved hearing your stories about this trip and how it changed your perspective so much. In a situation like that, do you get into a mental space where your only thoughts are around survival?

J: Firstly, I think survival is a mental state of mind. It's an acceptance of the environment that you're in and being able to adapt to your new environment. I think I did that well, as I've adapted to many environments in my life. Once you've adjusted it's then – 'okay, now let's survive this'. I think what happens in survival situations is we naturally adapt. I didn't try and put myself in a mental survival state, I just went into it. It's about connecting mentally and I suppose spiritually!

F: Did you stop worrying about the things that normally concern you when you're at home?

J: From the minute I stepped on the island, my phone, my bills, TV, house, car – all became a distant memory and the only thing that I thought about was the love I have for all my family. As I was fishing, filtering water, looking for food and cooking, I thought, how lucky am I to have such a beautiful family? I really did!

F: When you came over to the house shortly after your arrival home you explained so beautifully about those moments of silence you would experience. You would be on fire duty, making sure the much needed fire didn't go out, while watching the sunrise. With no one else awake and just nature to enjoy you must have had quite a clear head I'm imagining?

J: Yes, my mind felt clear, it wasn't full of all the things I have to do back home. It was peaceful, calm with the sound of the sea and the birds – so good for the mind. Then when the day got going, we just had important things that needed to be done that day on the island: fire, water, food – simple really, but hard work every day. Who was going to fetch water, more wood for the fire, who's hunting or fishing that day, fixing the shelter, cooking – and was it going to rain? That was all you had to worry about. Surviving. So the mind wasn't cluttered with loads of things, people, noises, Chatter etc. that we have here.

F: Did you realise in these moments how important silence is?

J: It was never completely silent but the few things I heard on the island were beautiful sounds. The sounds of nature. So therapeutic.

F: How do you think nature helps with our mental health?

J: I think it grounds us – brings us back in tune with the earth and what's really going on.

F: What is the best thing you learned about the experience?

J: I have learnt I'm a real survivor, and I've learnt that I'm grateful for the people I have in my life .

F: Thanks Jo Jo. Love you.

Quiet Doing

Stillness doesn't have to be boring or contrived or obvious. You can find this space and quiet however best suits you. For me there are tried and tested ways of creating a little cheeky loophole in the rule book. Being still while moving and ermm . . . sort of doing. Bear with me – what I mean is an activity that brings stillness. It might not be that still to look at or partake in but with it comes stillness. Think of stillness as a state of mind to ward off that mental Chatter rather than it always being literally still. For me the most obvious is yoga. I can move and flow through an hour of my day, if I can make the time and space for it, and that mental Chatter is nowhere to be seen. I am physically and mentally only communicating with the movement in that moment. I park all other concerns and voices and let my body move slowly and in a controlled manner, while my thoughts only revolve around those physical feelings. Stillness without being still. Running and walking are other examples. Being outside whatever the weather, walking or jogging, allows a huge slice of stillness to come in to the mix. I have clarity, am aware of what is going on around me and the voices within quite literally jog on. BLISS! And on days where I am feeling physically exhausted, I listen to my body – and not the mental Chatter – and go for a slow walk with a mate rather than pounding already tired feet. In overriding my negative Chatter, I make the decision that is right for me that day.

When I paint, I am doing but with no goal. There will be an outcome that could be great or not but the process allows me to shut off from all other thought and ensures the mental Chatter gives me the space to be purely physical and emotional. I never regret taking time out in the evening to paint or doodle. For you, it might be sewing, swimming, gardening, writing. It matters not what it is, only that we allow ourselves the time to welcome in that space. Stillness doesn't have to be quite so still.

HELLO TO . . . ERLING KAGGE

Before I started writing this book I stumbled across a copy of a book called *Silence*. By this point I already had the name *Quiet* in mind for this book and knew exactly what I wanted to write about so this was a nice dollop of serendipity falling into my lap. The cover of this book alone makes me sigh with relief and its words spoke to me and my busy brain in a way which seemed to really connect. Erling Kagge is an explorer and publisher who penned this book after several solo expeditions across the poles and up Everest. He has lived large chunks of his life in extreme silence and solitude and has learned a lot from what can be found in this peace. I loved the book so much that when I was covering a show on Radio 2, I begged the producer to get him over from Norway for a chat. It just so happened that Erling was travelling a lot that week anyway so he made it live on air to talk all things silence. I didn't so much interview him but quizzed him for my own personal enjoyment and need. I wanted to truly understand what he had learned and desperately wanted to apply it to my own life.

Silence is usually the one thing I feel I'm really lacking in life. We usually view silence as a negative or a subtraction, but the way Erling spoke about it, it became something I craved more than anything. We had such a lovely chat and swapped email addresses after the show. As soon as I started writing this book, I knew I needed to dig out that scrap of paper with his email address as I had even more questions I wanted to throw his way. He is an expert in quiet and stillness and is an advocate for us all seeking out more.

F: What have you learned from silence and the quieter times in life?

E: The quieter I am, the more I hear. Silence has its own language. To speak is precisely what silence does and you should talk with it.

F: In today's culture noise is everywhere and we find it so much harder to find peace in a literal sense and also in a mental way. How do you carve out this time and peace in your life?

E: Sva marga – follow your own path. I had to use my legs to go far away in order to discover my own silence, but I now know it is possible to reach silence anywhere. Because silence is about getting inside what you are doing. Experiencing rather than over-thinking. Allowing each moment to be big enough. Not living through other people and your devices but fashioning your own silence whenever you run, cook food, have sex, study, chat, work, think of a new idea, read or dance.

F: When you have been on your brilliant and long expeditions and are faced with long periods of solitude, how do you keep negative mental Chatter at bay?

E: I am taking one step at a time and try not to think too far ahead. During my Antarctic expedition I pulled all the food, gear and fuel I needed on a sledge and never opened my mouth to speak. I shut up for 50 days and nights. I had no radio contact, nor did I see a single living creature for those days. I did nothing but ski south each day. Even when I got angry, about a broken binding or because I nearly slipped into a crevasse, I remained focused on my next step forward and I did not curse. Negative thoughts, lashing out, brings you down and makes a bad mood worse. That's why I never swear on expeditions. I think most people underestimate their own possibilities.

F: When you're in tricky situations during an expedition and feel scared or worried about something, how do you stay positive mentally without anyone else to talk to?

E: Yes, life is tough while climbing Everest, walking to the Poles, but living with three teenage daughters has taught me that girls who are around fifteen years old have a tougher life than me. My experience as a father is that mid-teenagers must be the unhappiest group of people on earth.

F: Why do you think that?

E: I did not belong anywhere when I was fifteen. Childhood was gone, adulthood seemed far away, my parents felt stupid, I did not have any good friends, I did bad in sports and was a loser at school. Silence came across as loneliness and boredom – I lacked a purpose and for a few years I felt like I was being held captive. Silence was like a sound, rumbling inside my head. I thought I was the only one – but later I understood this is also life.

When I wrote *Silence: In the Age of Noise*, my daughters were thirteen, sixteen and nineteen years, and I believe they sometimes felt the same. And the more they tried to avoid silence, to be with themselves, the more unhappy and lonely they looked. Noise came in the form of distracting sounds and images, and as their own fleeting thoughts. They were always accessible, and almost always busy. Everyone was the other, no one was themselves. The three of them tended to sit in front of a screen – alone – enslaved to their phone, as a consumer and at times as a producer, constantly interrupted. Things just got to be too much. The problem is that they carried on seeking increasingly more powerful experiences instead of pausing to breathe deeply, shut out the world and use some time to experience themselves. The idea that unhappiness can be avoided by constantly pursuing something new on your device, being available around the clock, snapping and clicking further, waiting for a response, watching something you haven't yet seen is easy to believe, but it is lie.

F: Why do you believe we all need a little more quiet in our lives?

E: We are all born explorers, but back home I still sometimes have a vague angst about something I can't quite put my finger on. Something which causes me all too easily to avoid being present in my own life. Instead, I busy myself with this or that, avoiding the silence, living through my phone. I send messages, put on some music, play with an app or allow my thoughts to flit about, rather than holding still and shutting out the world for a single moment. I think it is a fear of getting to know ourselves better. There is a whiff of cowardice whenever I try to avoid that.

F: Erling, thank you for plying us with your wisdom. I feel very lucky to have interviewed you, the King of Quiet, for this book!

Constant Noise

In this mad modern world, actual silence can be near impossible to find. As I type this I can hear my husband hosing down our parched garden, cars whining by outside the window, planes flying overhead on their way to Heathrow, floorboards creaking in my rickety old house. Noise is omnipresent and hard to escape so we have to find this stillness within. We can't point fingers at every other hectic and noisy human on this planet. We have to find that quiet in whatever way feels right to us and it'll usually be a solo mission. I'm practising this one now. I'm not getting irritated by the noises around me, I'm just letting part of my brain notice them and without judgement. They're not negative sounds or positive, they're just there and perhaps this is how we can start to think about thought.

We will, of course, always have thought, negative and positive. These worries, concerns, excitements, memories and fears will come and go like the tide rolling in throughout our lifetimes, but if we just learn to notice them then let them go, we can live side by side with the inevitable. We can find our quiet and still even in a busy, mad world and create our own version of what that looks like. Find your own stillness and enjoy every minute of the clarity and quiet it brings.

I am not afraid to be still or of what I might find there.

Quiet

I have learned a lot through writing this book. I've changed my mind several times on it all as I've observed my own struggles with my negative Chatter. I've also gained great perspective and knowledge from the incredible people I have interviewed.

Throughout this process, I have been mentally tested, as such close self-analysis has been needed to write this book, and so my Chatter has peaked. Then, at times, I have practised what I'm talking about and experienced sheer blissful quiet. It's made me take note of those moments where I know I'm getting the good stuff; the peace of a simple walk in the park as the vibrancy of nature around me has pulled focus from any negativity.

I have managed to gain the quiet in moments of absolute chaos within the four walls of my own house. I have been able to watch my kids arguing over a Lego spaceship, spaghetti up the walls and a sink full to the brim and just STOP. Calm in the chaos and a lack of mental judgement about it all. I have found a corner of quiet in the most unexpected times, like when a stranger at my local swimming pool told me how much she loved my daughter's hair. A little moment of thanks without any mental Chatter: the simple transaction of kindness stopping me in my tracks.

Quiet is something I dodged massively growing up, like most teenagers and twenty-somethings. I wanted noise, angst, a cacophony of jubilant screams and wild, wicked laughter. Gigs, audiences, speakers up loud, the beep of a text message, the roar of a plane engine, the beating of my heart. I wanted to hear it all. I assumed there would always be something in it for me. Of course there can be and I have enjoyed so much noise over the years, but I am now learning to love the quiet. Proper quiet in my everyday life: a book read in a corner, a glimpse of the moon on a winter's night, swans gliding on the Thames. But also mental quiet. Space void of ideas, creation, worry and thought. A quiet that seems harder to reach but is always so worth it. I'm understanding the value in this quiet and how it actually helps me to create, think more clearly and worry less. Just as our bodies need rest after exercise, our minds do too. I get it at last! The world won't end if I stop thinking. I won't fail to exist if I don't have an idea every day. Bad things won't happen if I stop worrying. It's just the sound of my Chatter.

It requires some daily discipline, the propensity to be kind to ourselves and at times some good old fashioned determination, but we can quieten that inner monologue if we so choose. We will never be completely free of it, but I have certainly learned that I don't need to take it all quite so seriously, that everyone else is also experiencing it, too, and that I can still carve out big wedges of quiet in among it all.

Thank Yous

Although the majority of this book was written in spookily silent solitude, I have felt the support and love of those around me throughout, and for that I must give thanks.

For a start this book wouldn't be seen by a soul if it wasn't for Amanda and Emily at Orion Spring. I feel lucky and chuffed to bits that you guys publish my books and love our friendships that have grown from working with each other. Amanda, you are the most masterly catalyst when it comes to getting a new book out of me. Just when I think that I've dried up and have run out of ideas, you push me gently in the right direction and ignite my enthusiasm and determination once again. Emily, thank you for cheerleading me on all the way and laboriously checking through every word written with care and diligence. Ladies, I simply could not do it without you and certainly could not be in better hands.

Thank you to my manager Holly Bott at JM&U Group who receives on average 10 emails/WhatsApps daily from me asking for confirmation that I'm not losing my mind/cocking up my career. Thank you for your patience, spot-on advice and clarity on all things life/work, all whilst looking effortlessly cool in varying Adidas trackie tops. Mary AKA Maz with the best shoes, thank you for believing in all of my projects and helping me to maximise their potential. I'm forever grateful for your energy and words. Thank you to Sophie at James Grant for helping me run my life as smoothly as I can whilst juggling on average 10 different jobs and my hectic family life. Always so appreciated! Thank you to Rachel Mills at Furniss Lawton for keeping me on track with my deadlines and encouraging my writing career.

I'm forever grateful that I was able to offer up a full-bodied perspective on all things Quiet due to the beautiful brains I got to quiz for this book. Sarah McKay, thank you for your clear demystifying of the human brain in the context of this book. Invaluable!

To Giles Yeo for helping us all to connect the dots between the gut and mind. Truly fascinating and a great launch pad for a big chunk of this book.

Thanks to Billie Piper for the most brilliantly frank interview for this book. It's been such a trip watching your career expand into such diverse areas over the years, I'm in awe of your talent.

Dustin Lance Black, how you managed to string a sentence together let alone an inspiring and honest account of how you feel about this subject with a newborn baby in hand is beyond me. Thank you for your time and wisdom on this one and big kisses to little Robbie!

Dawn O'Porter otherwise known as Dawnio, I'm not only so grateful for your words within this book but also for your friendship. I have so enjoyed our pen-pal adventures throughout the years and the occasional cup of tea when you've made it back onto British soil. PS your aunty's honey is the best!

A big thank you to Rozanne Hay for such great advice on all things sleep. I will most definitely read those answers again and again in the hope that I keep my good sleep on track.

Thanks to Granny Jo for an insightful account of all things quiet after such an extreme trip to The Island. I'm still not sure how you managed 28 days surviving in such a way, or how you were more worried about what your hair looked like un-straightened rather than the fact there was NO FOOD! You are amazing.

Thank you Erling Kagge for your total expertise on this subject. You were the perfect person to interview for this book and once again your words have resonated with such potency and vigour. Jesse and I will get out to that fresh Norwegian air at some point, I promise.

Thank you to Clare for such an exciting chunk of the book on dreams. I found your answers fascinating and I now take much more note of my weird and wonderful mental adventures each night.

This book would certainly not look anywhere near as pretty as it does without the skilled hands of my great mate Jessie May Underwood. I'm not sure how but on each book you bring my thoughts to life with your watercolour illustrations and add fantasy and depth to what I'm waffling on about. I love you angel girl. Thanks also to the design team at Orion – especially Abi and Helen – for putting all these pages together so expertly.

A heartfelt thanks is also needed for my ever patient and tolerating family. Jesse, I know I can be a right pain in the arse when I'm in writing mode as my insomnia often peaks and my anxiety rockets along as I worry about every word I've written. Thank you for your time and space so I could get all of this out of my head and on to my laptop. Thank you to Rex, Honey, Arthur and Lola for being my best teachers in life. You are a constant reminder to live in the now, appreciate each day and to try again when things go wrong. I love you all to the moon and back.

Lastly, thank YOU! If you have also read *Happy* and *Calm* I am almost bashful with my gratitude that you have come back for more. I'm so glad that my words have connected with you and that you were intrigued enough with this one to give it a go too. If this is the first of my books you have read then welcome along! Cheers for listening to my thoughts, feelings, worries and concerns. I hope they have been helpful in some way or have made you feel less alone in your worries. One thing I have learned from all of these books is that we are all in this together.

Huge love to you all and a big fat THANK YOU!